WALKING THE LEADERSHIP LEDGE ENDORSEMENTS:

"Packed with practical tools and real-world advice, this book is a valuable resource for both new and seasoned leaders. I found insights I could use immediately—and it's one I'll keep coming back to."

—Jamie Stout,
Manager of Colleague Relations
and Compliance, Memorial Health

"I am excited to share this insightful book with every leader in my organization! It's an empowering, hands-on guide that provides easy-to-apply strategies to help you grow into a confident leader, regardless of where you are on your leadership journey.

—Christine Novaria,
Director of Human Resources,
M. J. Kellner Foodservice

"This book is chock-full of useful, practical information. It's real talk that I wish I had read when I started as a leader."

—Jennifer Bettis, CFRE,
Director of Development,
University of Illinois Springfield

WALKING THE LEADERSHIP LEDGE

The "NEW" Leaders' Guide to Building Resilience and Confidence at Every Step

TESS FYALKA

Published by
Hybrid Global Publishing
333 E 14th Street #3C New York, NY 10003
Copyright © 2025 by Tess Fyalka

Fyalka, Tess
Walking the Leadership Ledge: The "New" Leaders' Guide to Building Resilience and Confidence at Every Step

ISBN: 978-1-938015-03-8 (Print)
ISBN: 978-1-938015-04-5 (eBook)

Cover design by: Julia Kuris
Copyediting by: Wendy Pecharsky
Book Interior and eBook design by: Amit Dey
Author photo by: Josh Ryder

Website: www.anglecoaching.com

Disclaimer
The information provided in this book is intended for entertainment and general informational purposes. Some stories reference real individuals and companies, while others have been adapted or amalgamated to illustrate broader principles and ideas. Readers are advised to consult with a licensed professional before making any investment decisions. The author and publisher assume no liability for financial outcomes resulting from actions based on the content of this book.

DEDICATION

To Eric – My beloved partner on this labyrinth of life.

To Lauren and Aaron – May you live, love, and lead with joy and compassion.

To the Soul Sisters – The wise women who've walked alongside me.

FOREWORD

Leadership isn't a destination—it's an ongoing evolution that challenges you to become more than you thought possible. You are embarking on a journey of leadership, which is really a journey of growth personally and professionally.

Whether you've been thrust into a leadership role unexpectedly or you've been climbing the ladder for years, the landscape of effective leadership continues to shift beneath our feet. What worked for leaders a generation ago simply doesn't cut it in today's complex, interconnected world. **You could not have chosen a better guide on this journey than Tess Fyalka, and this book will help you navigate that new terrain with confidence and authenticity.**

Why Tess and why this book? Tess brings something rare to the leadership conversation: She's lived it, breathed it, and most importantly, she's helped others discover their own leadership potential in ways that feel both practical and transformative. Her approach isn't theoretical—it's battle-tested. She understands that leadership development isn't about adopting someone else's style wholesale, but about discovering and refining your own authentic leadership voice.

She's written the roadmap to becoming the leader you need to be, and she's done it with humor, wit, and wisdom. It's especially for you if you've been thrown into the role without much preparation. That doesn't mean you're not capable of being that leader; it means, perhaps, that no one has given you much guidance, and that's where this book comes in.

The reality is that most of us stumble into leadership roles without a manual. One day you're an individual contributor, and the next day you're responsible for a team, a budget, and outcomes that extend far beyond your own productivity. This sudden shift can feel overwhelming, but it's also where your greatest growth opportunities lie. Tess understands this transition intimately and has crafted this book to be your companion through those early, uncertain days and beyond.

Modern leadership demands vulnerability, emotional intelligence, and the courage to admit when you're learning alongside your team. It requires you to create psychological safety where innovation can flourish, while maintaining accountability for results. This balance—between being supportive and demanding excellence—is one of the most challenging aspects of contemporary leadership.

The best leaders I know are perpetual students. They approach each new challenge with curiosity, rather than defensiveness. They ask better questions instead of pretending to have all the answers. They create environments where their team members feel empowered to contribute their best thinking, not just execute orders from above.

The truth is that you can be a "new" leader at any stage in your career. For example, a marketing executive I worked with was new to a company that expected their leaders to develop the people around them. Yet he was used to being the ultimate guru of marketing campaigns. He was willing to explore being that kind of developer of people, but he was always weighing it against being the expert and final decision-maker on all their campaigns. He wasn't quite sure if he was ready to give up the throne. He liked being the "answer man." Today's leader is being asked to humble themselves in the name of ushering and guiding the team's success.

This executive's struggle represents a pivotal moment that many leaders face: the choice between personal recognition and team development. The old model of leadership, where authority came from being the smartest person in the room, is giving way to a new paradigm, where leadership effectiveness is measured by how well you elevate others. This shift requires not just intellectual understanding but emotional maturity and genuine commitment to others' growth.

I recently came across a definition of leadership that resonated with me deeply. It's from Ron Tite's book *The Purpose of Purpose,* and it says: "Leadership is taking specific action based on the information you have before you to improve the lives of those around you."

This definition captures something essential about leadership that gets lost in discussions about strategy and tactics: At its core, leadership is an act of service. It's about making decisions that benefit not just the bottom line, but the people who make that bottom line possible. When you embrace this perspective, leadership becomes less about wielding power and more about stewarding potential.

Tess, being the leader she is, designed this book to equip you to become that kind of leader – collaborative, purpose-driven, servant minded, and highly effective. It will change you, and how you choose to lead, for the better.

The following pages ahead contain more than advice—they contain the path to transformation. Tess has distilled years of leadership experience, both her own and that of the countless leaders she's mentored, coached, and trained, into practical wisdom that will serve you throughout your leadership journey. Prepare to be challenged, inspired, and equipped for the meaningful work of leading others toward their highest potential.

Laura Berman Fortgang, MCC
Executive Coach and Author of *Take Yourself to the Top*

CONTENTS

INTRODUCTION

I recently googled the definition of the word *leader*. And then I laughed out loud. Here are a few of the first results to pop up: "The person leads or commands a group, organization, or country." "The one in charge." "The person who convinces other people to follow." "A person in control of a group, country, or situation." "A person who has commanding authority or influence." These twentieth-century notions of *controlling, commanding, convincing, and in charge* are remnants from a bygone and far less complex era.

Then there's midcentury leadership expert Abraham Zaleznik's 1977 take on leadership. He asserted that leaders were more like artists—daring, visionary, and motivational, crafting, and communicating captivating missions and strategies. On the other hand, managers, those seemingly lowly second-string contributors, were viewed merely as executors whose focus was on coordinating people and tasks. In other words, the folks who got the work done.

There are the fabled leaders like Ernest Shackleton, upon whom *entire* leadership courses are built. We soak up his heroics with awe, wonder, and lofty admiration. Shackleton's British expedition ship, *Endurance,* was crushed by ice in the frozen waters of the Weddell Sea off Antarctica and sunk on October 27, 1915. The famed Antarctic explorer and twenty-eight crew survived despite brutal conditions and devastating obstacles. He is recognized as a motivating and inspiring leader who put his men first.

However, the crises he faced were largely of his own making. Don't get me wrong; he did engage in epic and remarkably successful efforts to save his men. But the guy ignored warnings from maritime experts about hazardous ice conditions. He didn't hire, train, or equip his crew to succeed. In fact, he selected many of the sailors for this transarctic expedition based on personality, putting people into jobs for which they had zero experience. Take Leonard Hussey, for example, an anthropologist and archeologist, who was assigned the role of meteorologist because he "looked funny" and could play the banjo.

Shackleton might have been loved and adored as a great adventurer, but the guy was not strategic in his planning, his hiring, or in setting a course for the success of his team or his objectives. In fact, his goal to reach the South Pole failed four out of four attempts.

Thankfully, your struggles are unlikely to be on the same level as Shackleton's, but there will be days when it feels like you, too, are stranded in the ice floes of the Antarctic. And you will stand toe to toe with the reality that leadership is far different than its many storied myths.

Leadership isn't dreamy or romantic. It would be nice if you could simply follow Zaleznik's philosophy and spend your days pondering the esoteric nuances of your next motivational speech that will inspire your team not merely to build a boat, but to sail the vast and magical seas.

In reality, being a leader doesn't guarantee you get to control, command, or even be the authority. It is challenging on levels you've never known. It requires skills—professional, technical, leadership, managerial, interpersonal—unwavering values, and a willingness to fully embrace and commit to continuous learning.

As a new leader, you will need humility, perseverance, and a good night's sleep as you face the many opportunities and challenges that lie ahead, including:

- Defining roles and tasks
- Establishing clear goals and expectations
- Strategically thinking, planning, and acting
- Connecting the work of the team to the larger mission and goals of the organization
- Creating an environment where team members feel they are valued and their work matters
- Having challenging conversations
- Providing real feedback
- Navigating interpersonal dynamics
- Addressing bad behavior
- Appealing to different workstyles
- Providing opportunities for professional growth and development
- Facing setbacks and disappointments
- Consistently being a source of hope
- Leading up, down, and across

Just to name a few …

No question about it, as a new leader, you've got your work cut out for you. But like most great adventures, as you walk the leadership ledge, you will discover what matters most, who you are at your core, what you stand for, what energizes you, as well as what deflates you. And, hopefully, along the way, you will have a meaningful impact on those you serve as their leader, manager, guide, and compass. I will be with you along the way. And in the pages of this book, you will meet leaders just like you.

Author's note: All leaders and their stories in the book are true. Names and other identifying information have been changed to protect confidentiality.

CHAPTER 1

THE DIRTY LITTLE SECRET

"What I essentially did was to put one foot in front of the other, shut my eyes, and step off the ledge. The surprise was that I landed on my feet."

—Katharine Graham,
publisher, *Washington Post*

It's official! You got the promotion! You're a LEADER! Yay! Let the celebration begin. . .or not.

I have a dirty little secret to share with you: Chances are, you didn't get the promotion because the organization knew you would be a fantastic leader. I'm sorry if that feels like a crushing blow, and it doesn't mean that you can't *become* a fantastic leader. It's just that you likely are not that person today, at this moment.

They (the powers that be) are probably simply hoping and praying that when you get tossed into the deep end of this turbulent pool known as leadership, you can figure out how to keep your head above water and manage not to pull anyone else under, should you not be able to surface yourself.

Why, you ask, do I have such a seemingly pessimistic attitude about your arrival to the big leagues? Actually, I have the utmost confidence in you and what you're capable of achieving. After all, you now have at least one book in your leadership library. And I sincerely encourage you to become a voracious consumer of all things leadership—books, podcasts, YouTube videos, Instagram, TikTok, coaching, mentoring, training, and whatever other means you have to develop your skills. The leadership development journey may begin here, but it will not end until you've said goodbye to your last team, whenever and wherever that may be on the long and hopefully fulfilling road ahead.

Nonetheless, it's quite likely you were awarded the promotion to a leadership role because you were really good at the job you had as an individual performer. In fact, you were probably crushing it, and because of your stellar performance record there's a Cubs' fan's level of optimism among the higher-ups that, somehow, in some way, you will be able to create the team you now lead in your high-performer image.

But here's the challenge you're facing: You know in baseball when the pitcher has to go to bat, and there's that embarrassing bunt because they haven't developed the batting skills necessary to knock it out of the park—or even to first base? They are still a brilliant pitcher, but an incredible batter, they're not. Similarly, to be an effective leader requires a whole different set of skills than those you've been using as a brilliant individual performer. But the good news is you can develop them…if you choose to. If you do, you can become as brilliant a leader as you are an individual performer.

High Hopes Hang on High Potential

Sam is a fantastic member of the accounting team. In fact, her accuracy rate is second to none. Her spreadsheets are spectacular, like poetry in numbers. They're mathematical workhorse geniuses. In fact, the joke in the office is that Sam could write an Excel formula to wash the dishes—she's that good. Sam is highly detail-oriented, and some would say controlling. But this has served Sam very well in getting important tasks done and following procedures. It has earned her high praise and recognition. The leaders in the organization believe that, if Sam is promoted to manager of the accounting team, EVERYONE around her will be just as good as Sam.

So, Sam gets the promotion. She's now leading the accounting team. At first Sam is confident that she will have no trouble making the transition. After all, it just means that she has more power and more control. Now she can make sure things are done the right way—her way.

Sam quickly realizes that being promoted to leader of the department was not a coronation. In fact, if anything, she feels her expertise carries less weight than ever, except for maybe on her first day on her first job her first year out of college.

She now has multiple stakeholders to answer to—direct reports, colleagues, bosses, internal and external clients—whose opinions, experiences, needs, and directives must all be considered, and often these stakeholders have competing agendas. Adding to her growing list of lamentations, she now has to give feedback, deliver performance assessments, have difficult conversations, and the list goes on.

She misses being able to focus just on the numbers—those beautiful uncomplicated black-and-white numbers in their nice, neat, tidy, straightforward columns and rows. Those were the days. She knew how to measure, quantify, and calculate success. She could clearly tally her wins and her losses. She was respected for her technical knowledge. Now several days will pass before she feels like she's getting anything done, let alone contributing anything meaningful to the department. And the last time someone told her she was doing a good job ... well, it's too long ago to remember.

She walks into her new office, closes the door, and sobs, "What have I done?"

"What Got You Here . . ."

Sam struggles to transition from individual performer to leader, and for good reason. There are five leadership dimensions—Relating, Self-Awareness, Authenticity, Systems Awareness, and Achieving—and eighteen leadership competencies within those five dimensions[1]—that stand between Sam, the brilliant individual performer, and Sam, the brilliant leader. Her technical prowess got her noticed. But in the immortal words of Marshall Goldsmith, "What got you here, won't get you there."[2]

Many new leaders step into their roles, holding on hopefully to a few long-standing and generally unhelpful fantasies that are quickly upended by facts:

	FANTASY	FACT
Mindset.	I finally have authority.	Success is dependent on your ability and willingness to work effectively with others toward shared goals.
Stakeholders.	Direct reports and my boss.	Every department, customer, vendor, or other person/entity that you and your team interact with.
Control.	I'm the leader. I'm in charge. I have the answers. My team just needs to do things the way I do them.	Your "control" comes from empowering others. The answers come from tapping into your knowledge *and* the collective intelligence of those around you.

---

[1] Robert J. Anderson, William A. Adams, *Mastering Leadership, An Integrated Framework for Breakthrough Performance and Extraordinary Business Results* (John Wiley & Sons, 2016), 303–307.
[2] Marshall Goldsmith, *What Got You Here Won't Get You There: How Successful People Become Even More Successful* (New York: Hyperion, 2007).

Focus	Tell people what to do and how to do it the "right way"	Define the desired results. Empower, train, develop the team to execute. Provide ongoing constructive feedback. Get out of the way.
Challenges	Deliver results	Deliver results while operating in a state of near-constant change and balancing competing priorities.
Necessary competencies	Technical processes	Systems, teamwork, developing others, clearly articulating goals and outcomes … to name a few

Oh, the Places You Will Go and the Challenges You Will Face…

The view from the mountaintop is spectacular, but to get there often requires long and difficult journeys through the dark and difficult valleys.

Like Sam, you, too, are probably struggling with more than a few of the common leadership challenges—the valleys—listed below. Let's take inventory. Check all that apply, and feel free to add a few of your own:

- Your team members may be moving, but in different directions, and you don't know how to align them.
- You can't trust your team to deliver on what is needed/expected.
- You avoid giving feedback to your staff because conflict is uncomfortable.
- You do give feedback, but nothing changes, or the other person gets defensive.
- You don't ask for feedback.
- You have high turnover on your team.
- You feel like you are constantly putting out fires.

- You know you should have a "vision," but who has time for that fluff?
- You and your team struggle to set achievable goals.
- You struggle to deliver meaningful performance evaluations to employees.
- You've had little or no leadership development training or coaching.
- You know you could be a better leader, if you just had a few key tools.
- You are stressed because you feel that you are not measuring up as a leader for your team or your organization.
- You are not sure what specific skills and behaviors make a "good" leader.
- Other—Add your own below.
  - My top leadership challenges:
    1.
    2.
    3.

At different points on your leadership journey, you will likely face many of the challenges listed above, as well as others. Is it any wonder that stepping onto the leadership ledge feels daunting—if not terrifying?

Leadership—What Exactly Is This Thing?

So, what is this thing called leadership, which is seemingly so complex, nuanced, and challenging that there are more than ten thousand books on Amazon written about it and more than *five billion* references to it on Google?

There are some 850 definitions of leadership. In 2016, Inc.com[3] ran the article "100 Answers to the Question: What Is Leadership?" Here are a few they cite:

---

[3] Lolly Daskal, "100 Answers to the Question: What is Leadership?," Inc.com, March 28, 2016, https://www.inc.com/lolly-daskal/100-answers-to-the-question-what-is-leadership.html

"A leader takes people where they want to go. A great leader takes people where they don't necessarily want to go, but ought to be." Rosalynn Carter

"If your actions inspire others to dream more, learn more, do more, and become more, you are a leader." John Quincy Adams

"Leadership is unlocking people's potential to become better." Bill Bradley

"Leadership is a matter of how to be, not how to do it." Frances Hesselbein

Today, the question continues to be asked. According to a September 2024 article by McKinsey & Company, "What is leadership?" it is defined as a *"set of mindsets and behaviors that aligns people in a collective direction, enables them to work together and accomplish shared goals, and helps them adjust to changing environments."* [4]

Harvard Business School Professor of Leadership John Kotter explained it as *"the ability to influence others toward the accomplishment of some goal."*

Mary Parker Follett, often referred to as the "Mother of Modern Management" and a leadership visionary well beyond her time, noted, *"The most essential work of the leader is to create more leaders."*

All of those definitions capture important elements of leadership. I encourage you to begin thinking about your own definition. How will you define the leader you are becoming?

You Are Not Your Father's Leader…
If You Want to Succeed

As the cliché goes, there is nothing more constant than change, and what we call leadership has not been spared. While twentieth-century leadership built an industrialized and technologically advanced society, leaders

[4] McKinsey & Company, "What Is Leadership?," September 10, 2024, https://www.mckinsey.com/featured-insights/mckinsey-explainers/what-is-leadership

in that era were typically experts in their field who were and still are typically described as having exercised a command-and-control approach to get work done.

Twenty-first century leadership looks very different from its seemingly authoritarian predecessor. Successful leadership today is characterized by a more holistic and inclusive approach that emphasizes empathy, compassion, authenticity, adaptability, diversity, and collaboration. Leaders who embody these qualities are better equipped to navigate the complexities of the modern world and drive more sustainable success for their organizations and their teams.

The myth that the leader has or should have all the answers is a relic of the past, hearkening back to simpler times, when the manager on the factory floor had come up through the ranks and understood how the line worked from front to back. It's an impossible model to sustain in our complex and uncertain modern world, where change truly is a constant way of life and work.

Leaders who can quickly scan the landscape, leverage the significant talent around them, collaborate, and tap into the collective intelligence of their teams, organizations, and communities will be far more likely to thrive. These are the leaders who not only know, but willingly embrace, the fact that they do not have total control, nor do they have all the answers. They cannot merely force, will, or push their way to long-term success. It must be cultivated and nurtured over time.

They welcome and encourage varied and different perspectives and dialogue from a diverse cadre of colleagues, teammates, and stakeholders. They recognize quickly or are schooled, often promptly, that their ability to establish real and meaningful connection is central to their ability to lead effectively.

Ultimately, through the challenges, wins, painful losses, sleepless nights, and, yes, joy-filled days, the leader they were always meant to be, the leader that their organizations, communities, and society at large needs today—the 21st-century leader—emerges.

The Reluctant Leader

While some individual performers have leadership at the top of their list of goals right out of the starting gate and will actively look for opportunities to lead committees, projects, and special initiatives, for others, the calling of leadership is more akin to that annoying smoke alarm beeping at 3 a.m. They keep trying to ignore it, but to no avail.

Jacob's career is in workforce planning, where he leads a team of five direct reports. He transitioned from peer to team leader after watching six previous department heads come and go over the course of nine years. "Leadership was never on my radar. I'm a first-generation college graduate, and I was very happy working as an individual contributor," he says.

The revolving leadership door was exhausting and demoralizing. "Every time we would get a new leader in here and teach them what we do, they would leave for another promotion. It was like no one cared enough about the work to stick around long enough to do it, so I was asking myself how we move forward and take things to the next level."

Jacob was tired of teaching the ropes to the rotating cycle of department heads, so he decided to interview for the position himself, and he got it.

Growing Pains—from Peer to Leader

As an individual contributor, Jacob knew his work well, and having been in the department for several years, he had a general idea of others' responsibilities, but he knew there were gaps. "I feel like there's a perception as a leader that you're supposed to always have all the answers and know everything. There were areas I was now overseeing, where I didn't know the ins and outs. I had a lot of fear around that."

Jacob was stepping onto the leadership ledge and felt like his next move might just cause him to tumble over it. "For the first sixty days, I was like, 'What did I do?'"

But the biggest challenge came just a few months after Jacob moved into leadership, when the organization was facing layoffs. His small team lost a long-term team member. Compounding his challenges was a peer who struggled to accept Jacob as leader of the department.

Moving from peer to leader is a transition for the entire team, not just for the one getting the promotion. The person who was a peer and may have also been seen more as a friend, now holds significant power over their team members' livelihoods. Some new leaders see their role as one of power and control. They believe they need to exercise both to get the team "in line" or keep them there.

Reluctant leaders, those who suddenly find themselves in leadership positions, may take the opposite approach, seeking to maintain comfort in the role of the friendly fellow team member—that is, until a challenging situation, a tough decision, or a performance issue arises. That's when their leadership mettle is tested.

Team members might assume that since their new leader is a former team member, they'll look the other way when certain rules are bent, or shortcuts are taken. After all, they were once part of the team, right? Yes, the new leader was once a team member, but the team members most likely don't know what it's like to walk a mile in the new leader's shoes.

Establishing expectations early on and sharing your leadership philosophy right out of the gate helps let the team members know where you stand. What's important to you? What do you value as a leader and a person? What does your new role need from you? What's your vision of what is possible for the team going forward, and how do you see each member succeeding within that vision?

Jacob struggled with a fellow team member, Alex, who, from Jacob's perspective, could not accept Jacob in his role as leader. "It got to the point where he just refused to do certain tasks because he felt they were 'beneath' him. And when I would talk with him about it, he had this strong sense of entitlement because he had been in the department for several years and felt that he should be promoted to a higher position. He didn't think he should have to do certain things. But he also hadn't demonstrated that he was willing to invest in his own development to be able to earn the promotion."

It wasn't working. As is often the case, one person's behavior has a powerful ripple effect across the entire team, especially when the team is small. Yet, Jacob saw himself as a servant leader whose job was to remove roadblocks, ensure that team members felt safe in sharing perspectives, ideas, opinions, and create stability, so that work could get done.

The roadblock was Alex. Jacob faced a team member who couldn't accept feedback and wouldn't take corrective action. "Alex never could understand where I was coming from and how his actions were impeding his success and impacting the reputation of the team. If it was my leader giving me this feedback, I would take it and do something about it."

As human beings, we tend to believe that everyone thinks the same way we do. Intellectually, we get that everyone is "different," but we also have a cognitive bias that causes us to see our own beliefs and behaviors as the "right" ones. So, it can be utterly shocking to us when the other person doesn't "get it," whatever "it" is, because "it" is completely obvious to us— as it was for Jacob. From his perspective, Alex was refusing to accept the feedback and act on it.

Alex may well have believed that he was underutilized, and his time would have been better spent on other activities, and he may not have been able to articulate that in a way in which Jacob could "hear." The two would have been talking past one another and likely digging in, but we'll never know, because, after several months, Jacob felt he had no other options but to remove Alex from the team.

With the layoffs, the organization was in turmoil, and Jacob's leadership skills continued to be tested. Across the company, people were leaving, and the climate was rife with uncertainty and anxiety. "It got to the point where I was getting tired of explaining to people, 'Hey, this person's gone, but don't panic.' And all these departures were coming on the heels of the layoffs," Jacob says. "I just kept having conversations and encouraging team members to come to me. I didn't want them stewing and worrying. I tried to be fully transparent. 'Things aren't great, but this is what we're doing and here's how you can help.'"

Proving Ground

Along the way, Jacob realized that this was why he wanted to step into a leadership role in the first place. "I had seen and experienced so much transition turmoil in all the leadership changes we had. I know the work. I have a long history with the organization. I believe in the mission. When I took the position, I believed that I could provide some consistency and stability and help the team get to the point where we could really focus on the work and strategically moving forward."

Jacob says the challenging first year as a leader was kind of a proving ground for him. "I was proving to myself that I could do this. Just because leadership wasn't on my radar didn't mean that I wouldn't be successful at it. Now I can help move the team and our department forward."

As Jacob quickly came to realize, leading his team wasn't about magically having all the answers. Rather, he had to lead his team through times of turbulence and change. He had to set a vision for what was possible. He had to align his team to the vision and make difficult decisions about who would and would not stay on the team.

Responsible for 80 Percent of the Workforce

Most new leaders, even reluctant ones, eventually dream of leading flourishing departments, projects, teams, and organizations in which their employees are delivering on a clear mission. They have a sense of purpose and are serving their customers and communities with excellence.

But too often that dream is lost in the day-to-day challenges of high staff turnover, interpersonal conflict, communication breakdowns, and ineffective problem-solving. Each of those challenges is a symptom of the larger issue: poor or ineffective leadership and little to no leadership development training.

Leaders who have not been trained to set clear expectations, foster teamwork, provide feedback, navigate challenging conversations, or effectively coach their employees often experience high turnover, poor results, and very high stress. And yet, it is these leaders, many who stand on the front lines, who are responsible for more than 80 percent of an organization's workforce and successfully executing the business' strategy.[5]

It's a vicious cycle, and it's especially challenging for smaller organizations that often do not have the resources to pursue or effectively implement leadership development programs. As a result, the vast majority of employees promoted to leadership or management positions are unprepared.

A recent study revealed that for those promoted to leadership, 84 percent found the move to be stressful, and 90 percent said they felt unprepared, while 40 percent weren't sure it was the right decision.[6] Yet, the success of the business is inextricably linked to the effectiveness of these leaders.

---

[5] The Frontline Leader Project, Exploring the Most Critical Segment of Leaders, Development Dimensions International, Inc. 2019 p.3

[6] The Frontline Leader Project, Exploring the Most Critical Segment of Leaders, Development Dimensions International, Inc. 2019 p. 42

Unprepared leaders/managers fuel employee disengagement and attrition. The old adage "Employees don't quit jobs, they quit managers" lingers. In fact, survey research from Development Dimensions International revealed that a full 57 percent of people quit a job specifically because of their boss, and another 32 percent seriously considered it.[7] Worse yet, replacing an employee has been estimated to cost up to four times their annual salary, depending on the position.

I dare say that the world needs effective, values-grounded, people-focused, data-informed leaders now more than ever. The responsibility is often well beyond challenging. It can also be well beyond rewarding. You truly do have the opportunity to have a profound and powerful impact on those around you, your organization, and most importantly, your community.

What to Expect from This Book

My hope is that this book will help you on your journey. Does it have all the answers? Of course not, but it will give you specific and actionable steps you can take, skills you can develop, and resources you can use on your leadership journey. And you will need them—and many more, because there will be days when you feel like you are teetering on the ledge, and some of those days will see you tripping over it and falling into the abyss. But you'll have at least a few tools to grab onto, climb up, get back on course, and continue to collect additional tools along the way.

We will explore both the "being" and the "doing" of leadership. How you choose to be in relation to your team, your stakeholders, your community, is every bit as important and impactful as what you actually get done—the results you deliver—and for very good reason. Your ability to get the important work done, achieve your goals, move the dial, and

---

[7] The Frontline Leader Project, Exploring the Most Critical Segment of Leaders, Development Dimensions International, Inc. 2019, p. 59

deliver what is expected of you is dependent upon the quality of the relationships you build with the people you rely on to help you make it all happen now that *you* are a "leader." Each of those relationships is built through genuine connection.

We'll also cover key topics, including setting clear expectations, delivering feedback, having difficult conversations, building relationships, navigating challenging team dynamics, living your values, and better understanding when it's time to walk away.

In the upcoming chapters, you'll meet more "new" leaders like Sam and Jacob. And it's likely that some of the leaders you will encounter in this book are much like you—facing challenges, enjoying wins, recovering from painful mistakes—doing their best as they walk the leadership ledge. They, like you, are trying not to trip, slip, stumble, and fall, yet they, too, learn to heed these powerful lessons when they do.

CHAPTER 2

THE DEVIL IS IN THE DERAILERS—TRAPS LEADERS SET FOR THEMSELVES

"Failure is not fatal, but failure to change might be."

—John Wooden

Kate reviewed the results of her leadership competencies self-assessment. She shook her head and closed her eyes to escape the harsh reality of the data spread before her. "This is not the leader I want to be, and it sure as hell isn't the leader I need to be."

Kate is in a new role as vice president for a nonprofit organization. She's been highly successful and has led multiple teams and departments during her career. But this VP role in a new and larger organization has been a huge disrupter for Kate. Nearing her one-year anniversary, she knows she hasn't delivered as the highly competent leader they expected when they hired her. She is angry and frustrated. The results of her assessment have simply confirmed what she's seen in herself over the past several months. She's been holding back, seeking approval, asking for permission, rather than pursuing outcomes and setting forth a clear vision.

There are multiple ways in which new leaders can tumble over the leadership ledge, and one of them is playing it too safe. It's often described as "playing small," playing not to lose, or being too passive or compliant. It's an excellent example of how behaviors that serve individual performers well can trip them up when they become leaders or are promoted to higher-level positions.

The "My Only Concern Is for Others" Lie

Those who play it safe rarely rock the boat. They often describe themselves as pleasers, and that helps them convince themselves that their behavior is, indeed, virtuous. After all, they tell themselves their chief concern is making sure everyone is happy. As team members, they are often adored because they get along well with others. They steer clear of conflict and generally don't push their opinions too strongly, so as not to ruffle others' feathers. Their relationships and being seen as kind and friendly are extremely important to them and their identity in this world.

Now, some of you may be scratching your head and thinking, *So what exactly is wrong with this behavior? While others may find your hair standing on end at the thought of not addressing challenges promptly, radically, and with force.*

Let me be clear: There are many gifts that these "play it safe" individuals have to offer. For starters, they can be very emotionally intelligent and fiercely loyal. They pick up on the cues around them. However, those signals can become so loud that it paralyzes them as they struggle to make exactly the right decision, weighing the pros, the cons, and everything in between in hopes that the choice they eventually make will not disturb their much-desired peace and harmony, or, God forbid, upset someone.

They often build strong connections with their team members and can be genuinely concerned about them. All of this is very valuable in building an engaged team, but as a leader in service to the mission of the organization, the effectiveness of the department, and the leader's vision, there's a very important detail that sometimes must come at the expense of always being likeable: You have to get stuff done.

Though it's widely understood that you can't please all the people all the time, the compliant pleaser leader will do everything in their power to prove that truism is false, all the while gripping the handle on the leadership teeter-totter. They are either up and everyone loves them, or they are down, landing hard with a teeth-rattling jolt, and everyone hates them—or so they perceive. They struggle to comprehend that in between the "they either love me or hate me" polarities, there is a whole spectrum of possible actions, reactions, behaviors, and possibilities that can shape and define their full, and what could be a very effective, leadership approach.

For new leaders with a strong need for approval and a high focus on pleasing others, a sense of helplessness or a victim mindset can be another consequence that keeps them from having difficult conversations, setting clear expectations, and holding others—and themselves—accountable. They see themselves at the mercy of circumstances, situations, and people.

Isn't It Obvious?

Joseph recently purchased a franchise that specializes in high-end car products. He moved from working in insurance, where he was an independent agent with lots of autonomy and little experience in leading and managing others. Joseph was drawn to the franchise business because he really likes the products, as well as the idea of running a business. Although nearing age fifty, he, too, is a "new" leader.

As a new leader, Joseph is extremely frustrated with a few members of his team because they don't interact with customers the way he thinks they should. They bring drama and complain about one another. He rolls his eyes when he talks about a few of his employees. "It's so frustrating. How do they not see what needs to be done? I mean, isn't it obvious?" he asks incredulously.

But he's never told them what he expects. Joseph doesn't realize that the way he measures "excellent customer service" isn't necessarily the same way his employees measure it. He wants them to "just know," like osmosis. But that is only half of it.

The reason Joseph won't tell his employees what he expects is because he "hates having 'those' conversations," as if setting clear expectations is one of "those" conversations. You know, the amygdala-hijacking; fight, flight, or freeze; highly emotional; racing heart; and sweaty armpits kind of conversation.

Joseph's perspective around "those conversations" is akin to telling yourself that it might upset the waiter at the restaurant if you tell them that you want your steak prepared medium rare. The waiter not only wants to know how you want your steak prepared, but they also NEED to know so that they can do their job. And, no, it will not be obvious to the waiter from that side-eye of yours that charred, chewy, with ketchup on the side isn't the entrée you're hoping for. You are required to articulate your desires and expectations.

Similarly, Joseph's employees want to know and NEED to know what is expected of them so that they can do their job. Just because it is "obvious" to Joseph does not mean it is obvious to his team.

The Curse of the Crappy Boss

Joseph views this and most interactions with his team through a very narrow and blurry lens that I call the "Curse of the Crappy Boss." Joseph, like most of us, has had his share of horrible managers. One, in particular, had a profoundly negative impact on him. The manager would frequently berate employees for the smallest mistake. Joseph doesn't want to be "that type of boss." He doesn't want to be a boss at all. He wants to be a friend. Being a friend and being a boss are mutually exclusive in Joseph's eyes. He can either be a nice, friendly person or a jerk of a boss. His business and his team need neither.

If Joseph were to shift his perspective from being a boss to being a leader, he might find that he has stronger, more positive connections with his team and he can establish clear expectations, so they know what is expected of them. Instead, he clings tightly to a destructive and unhelpful identity: "I'm just a big, disorganized teddy bear."

Joseph is genuinely big-hearted and kind. He fears not being liked by others. It is a default position, which might become a derailer for him and his business, because it undermines his core strength: the ability to build strong relationships.

As the leader of his franchise business, he should be setting the vision or advocating for what is important for the business' success. He does not establish expectations, performance measurements, or provide much-needed and desired guidance for his team. Rather, he runs from team member to team member, making sure everyone is OK, glossing over issues, and being careful not to challenge anyone too forcefully. All the while, he hands his entrepreneurial dreams over to the illusion that if he just treads carefully enough, he will always be liked and adored by all. He might be liked right off the leadership ledge.

In their book *Mastering Leadership*, Robert Anderson, creator of The Leadership Circle 360 profile, and William Adams, make the case that the "Complying Dimension," one of the self-limiting reactive tendencies that stifle leadership effectiveness, has the greatest negative impact on leadership effectiveness, writing, "…this type of person tends not to push controversial issues, to be conflict-averse, and thereby fails to lead."[8]

---

[8] Robert J. Anderson, William A. Adams, *Mastering Leadership* (John Wiley & Sons, Inc, 2016), 188.

Tackling the challenges, addressing what's getting in the way, and achieving goals are central to leadership. For complying leaders, this is often a significant hurdle. "Complying seriously interrupts leadership effectiveness,"[9] according to Anderson and Adams. Leadership effectiveness requires setting a vision, pursuing challenging goals, building an excellent team culture, establishing clear expectations, and tracking revenue objectives. Leaders must be able to both relate effectively with their team and also achieve the goals of the business.

In other words, leaders who play small, roll over in the face of difficulty, don't establish clear expectations or provide feedback, struggle to achieve what they set out to do. They struggle to achieve the goals that are expected of them because they fear displeasing others. They compromise their dreams and desires because, in pursuing them, they might have to push themselves and others out of their comfort zones.

Constantly seeking the approval and acceptance of others is exhausting. It doesn't provide the emotional space or intellectual bandwidth to actually consider what your own vision is, or what your personal measure of success is. Living in a persistent state of fear of rejection leaves you stuffed tightly into the tiny jail cell of other people's approval. There's no room to move, let alone spread your wings and fly. As a result, you become more risk-averse, indecisive, passive-aggressive, and compliant, and that does a massive disservice to you, your team, and your potential.

Ultimately, Relationships Suffer

Worse yet, it undermines relationships, the very things that are so important to those who tend to be highly compliant and pleasing. By withholding, sugarcoating, and not addressing the alligators snapping at your and your team's heels, relationships and trust are compromised among your team members. They can't trust you to speak the truth. Critical issues are

---

[9] *Mastering Leadership*, 191.

left to fester, and team members can plainly see that their leader, while likeable and a "nice person," cannot be counted on to address the challenges ready to devour and derail them, the department, and quite possibly the business.

As acclaimed American novelist Toni Morrison stated in her 1993 Nobel Prize acceptance speech, "There is no safe way to be great and no great way to be safe." Walking the leadership ledge requires leaders to venture into uncertain, uncomfortable, and challenging territory.

What do you want to build, create, foster as a leader? What do you want for your team, your department, your organization, your business, your community? Yourself? What is the powerful impact that you can have on the other side of those difficult conversations? What could you build within the infrastructure of those clearly established expectations? And what might you inspire in those around you with the stirring vision you've strung in Post-it Notes above your desk? I dare say, a lot. Someone who naturally builds relationships is a powerful force when they recognize that they can, indeed, be both a likeable human being and a visionary high-achieving leader. The world needs leaders who can build effective teams and get stuff done. You, my friend, are halfway there!

> ### "Pretend inferiority and encourage his arrogance."
>
> ### —Sun Tzu, *The Art of War*

Liam likes to lift weights. His stocky muscular frame takes up space at the conference table. Spreading out in his chair, his pectoral muscles do a little dance under his polo shirt. Liam is hardworking, intelligent, and believes strongly that he is ready for a promotion. He is also cynical and sarcastic. He proudly says he is not one to "drink the corporate Kool-Aid."

As part of his leadership development plan, he was given 360-degree feedback, an in-depth review that assesses leadership competence. As a professional and a leader, there are few experiences as anxiety-producing.

Some believe they are an excellent tool for development, and others feel strongly that they do more harm than good. When the process is used for professional development, not as a performance review, it can shine a bright and necessary spotlight on the leader's blind spots. Everyone has them. Left unaddressed, these blind spots, Achilles heels, shortcomings, growth opportunities, whatever euphemism you give them, can throw leaders off track and over the leadership ledge.

For those who have the opportunity to experience 360-degree feedback in a psychologically safe environment in which they are provided with the coaching, tools, and training to grow and develop, it can be a profoundly positive life- and career-changing experience.

In the words of Scottish poet Robert Burns, "*O wad some power the giftie gie us, to see ourselves as others see us!*" Cracking open the door to better understand how we are experienced by our colleagues, teammates, and others can provide valuable insights into our behavior and character. It can also be quite startling. After all, we expect and want others to judge us by our good intentions.

So while the truth will set you free, it's most likely to first tick you off, trigger you, and quite possibly have you running for the exits to protect your ego from the sheer discomfort of coming face to face with your leadership struggles—the ones you know you have, but were really hoping that no one else happened to notice. I'm sorry to tell you they have noticed, and they are taking notes. If it's any consolation, I promise you that every single leader on the planet faces challenges, shortcomings, and areas in which they just plain suck. Welcome to the utterly fallible human race.

Liam pulls a taut half-smile across his face. His armor is on, and his shield is up, ready for battle. "Well, how bad is it?" he asks in a matter-of-fact tone that conveys his "you will never see me sweat" attitude.

He scored himself at 80 percent in the categories of critical, arrogant, and distant. On this, he and his twelve evaluators—peers, colleagues, boss, boss' boss, and others—essentially agree. They scored Liam at nearly 90 percent.

Liam prides himself on knowing his craft, and he has little patience for those he perceives don't care to know theirs or have the audacity to question him, his decisions, or his intelligence.

Upon reading a few of the comments from his evaluators, his jaw tightens.

> *"Liam resorts to force when vendors don't do what he wants them to do or don't do what he thinks they should be doing. He comes across as frustrated and angry. This doesn't help the situation."*

> *"When Liam doesn't get his way or someone disagrees with him, he's clearly irritated and just wants to be done with the conversation."*

> *"Liam projects frustration and irritation with the client."*

And there were many more, echoing a similar theme. Liam's shoulders nipped at his ears, and his face reddened. "It's just my personality, and in my role, I can't look weak or like I don't know what I'm doing."

Brené Brown may extol the many virtues of vulnerability. But for Liam, that word represents danger and feeling exposed and helpless. At this moment, he has no interest in standing at the vulnerability intersection where fear and courage are said to meet.

With regard to his overall effectiveness as a leader, Liam believes he is knocking it out of the park, crushing it, with a self-score of 83 percent. His evaluators beg to differ. According to them, his overall leadership effectiveness score clocks in at 13 percent.

Liam believes he holds high standards. He makes every effort to deliver with excellence, and expects the same from those he works with. And he is, indeed, respected for these attributes.

It is not all seemingly discouraging news for Liam. In fact, for every comment regarding what his evaluators experience as critical, arrogant, and distant behaviors, there were many pointing to his tenacity, goal orientation, likeability, and eagerness to learn.

His high standards are respected. They reveal his potential as not just a high performer, but eventually as a high-performing leader—if he can address the potential derailers. Much like a derailed train, leadership derailers can have a profoundly damaging effect on the leader, the team, and the organization.

Derailment—Disaster or Development?

While there can be many behaviors and circumstances that can send a new leader tumbling over the leadership ledge, it is often communication—the lack of it, too much of it, or the tone of it—that causes leaders—new and experienced—to be derailed. Below are seven key derailers—all rooted in communication. Obviously, this isn't intended to be a comprehensive list. Consider it a means of surveying your own landscape for the traps and tripwires you're setting for yourself on your leadership journey. Remember: Derailers don't have to spell disaster IF a leader is willing to acknowledge and address the behavior.

1. *Aloof*—You know when you're walking through the office and you're so focused on the problem you're solving in your mind, or the meeting you're heading to, or the list of 250 items on your to-do list, and you don't make eye contact or acknowledge any of the five people you've just passed? You reason that you simply don't have time for chitchat, small talk, and useless pleasantries. If you do this on the regular, you'll likely be communicating a message—intentional or not—that you prefer to keep people at arm's length. You'll likely be experienced as cold and distant. Aloof leaders prize data and analysis and prefer to deal with challenges on a strictly logical and rational basis. They typically lack

emotional intelligence, which eventually impacts their ability to effectively lead, foster teamwork, and build trust.

2. *Arrogant*—I'm betting that when you see the words "arrogant leader," someone comes to mind. This person must demonstrate that they are the smartest in the room. They are convinced that their knowledge, experience, opinions, and perspectives are superior to others'. They believe that everyone is in awe of their intellect, and, oh, do they want to WOW you. They are convinced that their solutions are the best, their beliefs are the right ones, and their ideas are the most original. They frequently speak first, seek to attract a lot of attention to themselves, and struggle when their ideas are challenged. They are unwilling to listen to feedback or differing perspectives, shutting down diverse opinions and alternative ideas. This behavior can create a toxic work environment and significantly hinder psychological safety on a team. Worse yet, it creates an environment of learned helplessness.

3. *Critical*—If you subscribe to the belief that "brutal honesty" is the best policy, you may be coming across as a highly critical leader. While high standards and expectations are not only honorable, but also necessary, critical leaders communicate these standards and provide feedback often in a very harsh or negative manner. Others experience this leader as one who is looking for what is wrong, never what is right. Critical leaders find fault and blame others. They are rigid and dogmatic. This leadership style can create a tense, stressful work environment, where team members feel micromanaged, unappreciated, and undervalued. More troubling, highly critical leaders, like arrogant leaders, can create a culture of "learned helplessness," where team members fear stepping up to the plate, undertaking challenges, or pursuing system improvements, because whatever they do will be criticized by the critical leader. Consequently, trust, creativity, innovation, and morale all suffer.

4. **Controlling**—If you're convinced that it's just easier to "do it yourself," you may be a controlling leader. Control can be one of the greatest areas of struggle for new leaders. After all, what got you noticed as an individual performer, in many cases, was your ability to get the job, the task, the sale, whatever the job requires, done and usually with excellence. These leaders often struggle to delegate effectively. They can see what needs to happen, and they want to drive the results across the finish line themselves.

Consequently, they don't engage others. They struggle to communicate openly and often withhold information. A leader who consistently withholds information, feedback, and praise risks creating a negative and disengaged work environment. When they do communicate, they are telling and dictating, rather than engaging and collaborating. They commonly micromanage their team and may insist on having final say over all tasks, projects, and processes. This is not scalable, and it is unsustainable. The effective leader is able to get work done through others while engaging them and tapping into the collective intelligence of the team. The controlling leader ultimately will become a bottleneck.

5. **Indecisive**—Fear often grips the indecisive new leader. After all, they were likely rewarded and recognized for following the rules, acting on orders, and not making waves. While most of the literally thousands of daily decisions you make are unremarkable, routine, and have little consequence, as a leader, making decisions, including difficult ones, is what you've signed up for.

The indecisive leader may assure themselves that good things come to those who wait, but, in the meantime issues fester, customers leave, stress increases, the team falters, and what may initially be a straightforward decision can morph into a complex systemic problem that negatively impacts a wide swath of key stakeholders. That said, given that we live in an age in which millions upon millions of pages of information and data are readily available, it can be easy for the indecisive leader to fall into the paralysis of analysis trap as they search for just the right answer. For those who struggle on this front, it can be extremely helpful to tap into various tools, such as a decision matrix, the Eisenhower matrix, stakeholder maps, RACI matrix, as well as daily journaling. As a leader, difficult decisions must be made. Some will be good, some will be bad, some right, some wrong, and everything in between.

6. *Perfectionist*—A perfectionist leader may also be a critical leader. They hold extremely high standards for themselves and others, often striving for flawless results in all aspects of their work. This type of leader may pay close attention to detail, have an intense focus on perfection, and be critical of anything that falls short of their exacting standards. While this mindset can drive excellence and quality in some cases, it also comes with drawbacks that can impact both the leader and their team.

This leader may be hesitant to try new approaches, to innovate, to experiment, knowing that in the new and untested there is risk of failure and a near guarantee that the experiment will be anything but perfect. Their relentless pursuit of perfection can also lead to procrastination and indecisiveness, as they may prioritize avoiding mistakes over taking risks or making timely decisions. This leader also struggles to praise their team members for any efforts short of near miracles. They justify their pauper's portions of praise with a dismissive, "I don't hand out participation trophies." Failure to provide praise and recognition for good work is demotivating. Yes, it should be sincere and for a job well done, but human beings need affirmation and a sense that their work matters. Lacking positive reinforcement, individuals are far more likely to feel unappreciated and undervalued, impacting their engagement and productivity.

7. **Passive**—Passive leaders, like Kate and Joseph mentioned at the beginning of the chapter, tend to prioritize maintaining harmony and avoiding conflict over setting clear direction and driving progress within their team or organization. Passive leaders may exhibit traits such as indecisiveness, passivity, and avoidance of confrontation. They may struggle to provide clear guidance or direction to their team, leading to confusion, lack of motivation, and a sense of aimlessness among team members. When a leader withholds corrective feedback, it can have a multitude of negative consequences for both the leader and their team, including a lack of clarity, confusion, mistakes, inefficiencies, lack of trust and low engagement, and the list goes on.

Tools and Tricks to Get Back on Track

Consider the seven behaviors listed previously. Most new leaders discover that they tend to rely on a few lingering tendencies that probably served them well when they were individual performers. If you were to honestly evaluate your own leadership and communication styles on a scale of 1 to 5 for each (1 meaning you never or rarely demonstrate this behavior, and 5 meaning you often or always demonstrate this behavior), which two or three categories did you score the highest?

Perhaps you think there's a good chance that you exhibit specific behaviors, but are not sure what those around you see. Seek input from a few trusted colleagues. Ask them to observe you in upcoming meetings or other exchanges. Tell them what you want them to pay attention to specifically. For example, if you believe that what you consider to be high standards may be coming across as critical to others, share the brief summary provided in this chapter and ask your trusted colleague to jot down a few specific examples of what they observe of your leadership skills in action.

Most importantly, when your colleague shares their observations with you, accept their assessment with two words: thank you. If you start justifying, explaining, and arguing with them, you've told them that you're not sincere in seeking to understand how others experience your leadership. You've potentially damaged their trust and lessened the chance they will provide you with candid feedback in the future.

Awareness is the first step. From there, identify a specific behavior that you would like to minimize. For example, if your colleague noticed that you criticize, shut down others, and frequently point out what's wrong before getting the full story, try slowing down and asking a few neutral questions, such as: Help me understand your approach? What do you think went well on this project? What would you do differently? Then listen and truly consider the person's responses. As the leader, you're making a genuine effort to understand the situation, helping the other person engage in critical thinking, and enabling the team member to discern how they would approach the situation differently the next time around. The potential for positive impact is far greater, and you are engaging with your team in a way they will appreciate and learn from.

Demonstrate a willingness to learn from your team and, yes, be vulnerable. Tell them you are working on improving a specific leadership behavior. Invite them to share one or two suggestions to help you improve this behavior. Thank them. Don't argue with them. Don't tell them their suggestions will never work.

Experiment with a few of the suggestions you receive. Practice with those that feel more natural at first and then try those that nudge you out of your comfort zone. Unless your behavior is so egregious that you have to significantly change it immediately, small steps and experiments will lead to greater change over time. You are developing a new behavioral habit, and habits are not formed overnight. Some days will be easier than others, particularly when you are under stress and may well go off the rails again.

That's okay. Simply pick up where you left off and extend grace to yourself.

Kate, Joseph, and Liam

Kate worked with a leadership development coach for several months and reclaimed her power as a leader. She gained clarity on strengths and values, as well as the many gifts her experience could provide the organization. She learned how to articulate clearly what she needed from her boss in order to thrive in service to the mission and vision, and she set forth an ambitious goal plan for herself and the team. They are on track to make this their most successful year yet.

Joseph joined a leadership mastermind group and a leadership training program where—if he sticks with them—he will develop both his core leadership competencies, as well as learn how to build key systems in his business.

Liam took the feedback to heart. He went on to meet with a leadership development coach for over a year. He actively worked to develop his skills in listening and connecting with others. He was able to lower his shield and seek first to understand where others were coming from, before habitually becoming defensive and pointing fingers. Over time, he became known for his ability to invest in his teammates and develop those around him. Like all of us as leaders, he is still a work in progress, and some days he acknowledges he is far more effective than others. But the organization has recognized and rewarded his strides as a leader with promotions and significant project opportunities.

CHAPTER 3

SINK, SWIM, OR GRAB A FLOATY

"Treat a man as he is and he will remain as he is. Treat a man as he can and should be and he will become as he can and should be."

—Stephen R. Covey,
The 7 Habits of Highly Effective People

"If they would just do their jobs, everything would be fine," said Will as he shook his head and rolled his eyes. Will is a leader in a small retail business with about one hundred employees. His features are sharp, and he's built like a distance runner, though he brags that the extent of his exercise routine is paddling in his pool on an inflatable raft to grab a beer from the Yeti.

Like many leaders in small organizations, he is responsible for both leading his team and doing the work. But truthfully, Will would prefer to just be "doing." He likes the work, specifically connecting with customers, which he's very good at. But as for connecting with his team, not so much. He laments the distractions and irritations of the responsibility. "Work would be great if it weren't for the people," he said, namely his direct reports.

With the help of AI, Will, and others like him just might get their wish, but for now, as a leader, at least part of his job is to get work done through others. And to do so without the use of any sharp, blunt, or heavy objects…preferably.

Will initially loved the *idea* of being in leadership—and the promise of a nice raise. But the reality is a very different story. As the demands grow, he feels increasingly unprepared and ill-equipped for the challenges being a director in his organization presents. He readily acknowledges that he is struggling. When it comes to leading his team, his response is something along these lines. "All they need to do is what I do, and they'll be fine. Read the job description and just do their jobs."

Well, at least they have job descriptions. Many small businesses sing a common refrain: "We don't need all that 'formal' stuff. We all just do what needs to be done. We're like a family." And yes, for a minute, that charming notion works—until it doesn't—and the ice bucket challenge of reality hits them squarely between the eyes. Suddenly, they face the jarring reality that if everyone's responsible for everything, no one is accountable for anything.

Meanwhile, "the family" is scratching their collective heads trying to figure out how to cut Margaret out of the tree and saw off the branch that is Jake because *they* are the "problem children." Ultimately, it's employee turnover, missed deadlines, low morale, high absenteeism, increasing expenses, and shrinking profits that typically shine a harsh, bright light on how utterly dysfunctional a "family" they are.

But back to Will. Like many new/newer leaders, he's doing the best he can with what he knows. He does what he's always done, and is still searching the skies for the answer to why his employees never seem to be able to deliver on what he wants or expects.

He has not learned what it takes to lead a team effectively because, like so many new leaders, he was put into a leadership position because he was a very good individual performer. He's had little to no leadership development training, but he is often recognized for getting the work done.

His annual bonus is not based on how effectively he's leading his team. It's not contingent on how successfully he's developing other emerging leaders in the business. It's not dependent on how empowered his team members are to take action, address problems, and think critically. Rather, it is based on whether the spreadsheet said his accounts made money and products were delivered on schedule. So, not surprisingly, developing, mentoring, coaching, setting clear expectations, and providing feedback slide their way to the bottom of his "to do" list.

And when he does attempt to focus on these things, he's trying to find his way in the dark, and smacking his shins painfully hard into the furniture along the way. Yet, as the business continues to grow, Will's abilities as a leader are going to be measured against more than just profits and losses. Don't get me wrong, profits and losses are certainly important. But they are brushstrokes on the canvas of effective leadership. How well his team functions, the relationships built internally and externally, the happiness of the clients and team members, the growth and development trajectory of his staff, as well as the number of employees who want to continue to be part of his team or are searching for the exits, are also essential in painting the full leadership portrait.

Bottom line: Like Will, the success of your team will have a profound and powerful impact on your effectiveness and reputation as a leader. They are your most important stakeholders. The only way you achieve your organization, department, or project objectives is through them. Ignore them, disregard them, minimize them at your peril.

"Man" Overboard!

Until recently, in Will's department, new employees were hired based on who they knew in the organization, likeability, and it didn't hurt if they had a clever answer to the question: "What's your spirit animal?" There was no established interviewing, hiring, or onboarding process. For the most part, the manager had to wing it—from start to finish.

On the employee's first day, they were shown to their workspace via the all-important path to the bathroom and kitchen, given a quick tour of the computer system, and were left with a friendly, "Let us know if you have any questions." The rest of the team quietly prayed that the new hire wouldn't screw up things too badly between now and their annual performance review, when they would find out *everything* they had been doing wrong on the job up to that point—if they didn't quit or get fired before then.

They weren't just thrown into the deep end of the pool; they were tossed overboard into the middle of the ocean.

Onboarding new hires into your department or organization is critical to their success—and your sanity. In a widely reported study by Brandon Hall Group, "Organizations with a strong onboarding process improve new hire retention by 82 percent and productivity by over 70 percent. Companies with weak onboarding programs lose the confidence of their candidates and are more likely to lose these individuals in the first year."[10]

In Will's department, the lack of an onboarding process wasn't intentionally malicious or some sick psychological experiment to test the new hire's resourcefulness. With a half-time administrator to assist with HR functions as their schedule allowed, hiring and onboarding responsibilities were left largely to the managers to navigate on their own. So it was simply assumed that if the new employee had what appeared to be "previous experience," they would be able to, you know, "figure it out, hit the ground running, get up to speed," and all that other good stuff.

---

[10] Madeline Laurano, *The True Cost of a Bad Hire*, Brandon Hall Group, Research Brief, August 2015.

After all, if they had what seemed to be a similar job at their previous company, surely they knew what needed to be done in their new role. And certainly, no one wanted to insult the new employee's intelligence and imply that they might not necessarily know what is expected of the seemingly similar job in this company.

It is not uncommon for decision-makers in small organizations to assume that if you've held the title "project manager," "executive assistant," "accounting generalist," "marketing specialist," or whatever the moniker, your responsibilities in the previous organization were essentially the same as what will be needed in the role you're being hired for.

I will often hear new (and not-so-new) leaders say, "Well, JoJo was a fill-in-the-blank at X Company, so they should know what to do. I don't want them to think I don't trust them."

But that is exactly what will happen when that new hire is on the job, and they don't/can't execute as expected—or rather—as assumed they would be able to. The hiring leader's trust in that new hire will disappear faster than ice on a summer day.

The trust will emerge for both of you—if you equip them. One of your most important roles as a leader is to set up new team members for success in your department—to onboard them. This is not a one- or two-day orientation in which they are signing paperwork and shown where to store their lunch or how to log into the Zoom room.

Onboarding a new hire is about assimilating them into your organization's and your department's culture. It goes well beyond the transactional paperwork requirements that come with every new hire. It may last ninety days to twelve months, depending on the position. The most important outcome in the onboarding process is that the new hire knows what is expected of them in this role, and they have a clear understanding of what success looks like in the job.

Throw Them a Floaty So You Don't Drown

There are numerous excellent resources on how to set up onboarding programs. For now, I'll hit on a few fundamental steps to take when welcoming a new employee into your department, and to help ensure that your new hire doesn't morph into the dreaded "bad" hire.

Onboarding begins with a structured interview process in which all candidates are asked essentially the same questions. Those questions should be informed by the job description, so you can assess how their previous experience applies to the role you're filling and the work you expect them to be doing. No assumptions here—you need to understand how their experience actually applies—or not—to the duties they will be expected to perform in this job.

Engage others who will work closely with the new hire as well. This enables you to gather multiple perspectives on the applicant's knowledge, skills, and abilities. If possible, ask the applicant to spend a couple of hours shadowing an existing member of the team who is performing the same or similar duties well. This also gives others in your department the opportunity to assess the candidate's interest, experience, and fit, and it allows the candidate to get a sense if this position is a good match for them as well.

Once the candidate is selected, don't wait until their first day to welcome them into your department and your organization. Start generating excitement the moment they accept the job offer. Here's a sample menu of steps you can take right away to engage your new team member and allay any new job remorse that might start simmering after they've said yes.

One to two weeks prior to the new hire's start date:
The Welcome Email

- Spell out a few key details. Such as:
  - Additional information about the organization, the department, vision, mission, values, team/organizational goals, your excitement about their joining your team.

- ○ Specifics about:
  - What time to be at the office or online.
  - Where to park and where/how to enter the building.
  - Who will greet them.
  - What to expect on their first day.
    - Provide a schedule of the day—who they will be meeting with, when, and the purpose of each meeting.
    - If they are in the office, include lunch with the team, the leader, or their onboarding buddy. Don't leave them to eat alone at their desk.
    - Remember to be flexible. Schedules change, be prepared to pivot as needed—but don't abandon them!
- Provide necessary paperwork to complete electronically in advance of their first day.
- Schedule training meetings with the new hire and the subject matter experts (SME), who will train them on key processes and systems in the weeks ahead.

The first day/week:

Below are a few key activities to integrate the new team member into your department and the organization. The specifics for your department will look different, but this list should prompt some ideas for you.

- Provide access to the employee handbook.
- Provide the building or office key card/access card.
- Tour the office/meet the team.
- Meet with information technology for instruction on the computer system and other equipment.
- Connect with manager/leader.

- Meet with their onboarding buddy—this is the person they can go to for answers to those questions they want to ask but may not be comfortable posing to their leader/manager.
- Meet with other department heads and specific team members to gain an understanding of other facets of the business (sales, marketing, operations, accounting, warehouse, shipping, etc.).
- Meet with senior leadership.
- Review list of company buzzwords/acronyms.
- Watch company video.
- Tour other relevant office sites.
- Complete electronic profile on the company intranet.
- Provide workspace supplies and materials/company swag/business cards.
- Review profiles about their team members and trainers/mentors on the company intranet.
- Review the Building Relationships Checklist and begin scheduling meetings. These are the people inside and outside the organization whom the new hire must meet within a specified time period.

And, most importantly ...

- Review the onboarding training plan. The training plan is essential to setting up the new hire for success.
- Share an overview of the training plan with the new hire in advance of their start date, if possible. The training plan reinforces that their decision to join your team was the best decision they could have made because you are already calming any fears they might have and you are demonstrating that members of your team are set up for success. Yay, YOU!

The Plan:

The training plan introduces the new hire to the key job functions and begins to define what success looks like for the specific position. It is based on the job description and should cover what the new hire needs to know to be successful in the next 30, 60, 90 days and up to 12 months, depending on the position.

Organize the training priorities into three categories:

- Overview—These are the items/areas that the employee should have a basic understanding/overview of in their role. Create a manageable list of three to five areas/items.
- Capable—These are tasks/responsibilities that they need to be capable of performing within a specific time frame to successfully fulfill their job duties. Again, keep it doable, start with five or six items. You can always add to these lists. But nothing will trigger panic in you and your new hire faster than creating an overwhelming list.
- Master—These are the specific job duties in which the new hire needs to achieve mastery within a specific time frame to be a high-performing member of your team. Like the other lists, start small. This list will grow with the team member, and remember, mastery takes time.

Defining your training priorities will help you focus on what's most important now and what can be woven in over the coming months. Next, drill down a bit deeper into a few specifics.

- Provide general information about what they will be learning under each item on your priorities list. What are some key skills that the employee will learn in their training to execute this task successfully.
- Don't boil the ocean. You're going for progress, not perfection. You can always add to and change the plan as you experiment, test, and get feedback from those who join your team.

- Explain how the training sessions will be delivered, such as self-directed learning programs, webinars, classroom trainings, videos, one-to-one trainings with a subject matter expert (SME), etc.

- Sidenote—It's very helpful to put a draft of the training plan together, then test it out with a couple of team members. Their input will undoubtedly help improve its design.

Tap the Organization's Brain Power

Don't try to do this alone! You can't and you shouldn't. Engage members of your team and others in the organization as SMEs in the onboarding process.

For example, if Betsy is brilliant at completing key processes, engage her in training the new hire on those processes. It shows that you value Betsy's expertise, ensures that the new hire is trained correctly in those areas, and it enables the new team member to build relationships in the organization more quickly. What's more, when you teach, you learn, and that further develops Betsy's professional and technical skills.

But don't toss Betsy and the new hire into the deep end, with no direction as to what should be covered in the new hire's training session. Without a plan and a few key objectives, both the subject matter expert and the new hire are likely to drown. The SME doesn't know where to begin and quickly becomes overwhelmed. The new hire doesn't know what's important because the SME probably turned on the firehose, trying to download all possibly relevant information they can think of.

Instead, use the Sample Onboarding Training Outline in this chapter. The simple guide covers four key areas: Objective, Outcomes, Context, and Content. Your outline will look different, but the sample outline will help you more clearly define your onboarding training sessions' structure and focus.

Less is more! From your list of training priorities, start with those specific areas that the team member must know to be successful in the next 30–60 days, and build from there. Keep individual sessions focused and no more than 45–60 minutes.

Sample Onboarding Training Outline Template

Job title:

Name: (name of module here—e.g. Purchase Order set up using YouGot-This Software Program)

Objective: Here, you articulate the purpose of the training.

- For example: The objective of this training session is to guide the team member step-by-step in completing ____X____ and/or understanding ____Y____.
- Or: The objective of this training session is to provide the team member with Z (an introduction, overview, step-by-step instruction of the software/system/process) used by our department/ company.

Outcomes: Here, you spell out *a few specific* outcomes that the training should deliver. Use the items below as inspiration and create your own brief list of outcomes. The only requirement is that they must be specific.

For example:

Upon completion of this training session…
- The team member will understand _____.
- The team member will be able to perform these tasks:
  o A
  o B
  o C

- The team member will be able to complete this process. . .
- The team member will know who/where to access the information they need to do X.
- The team member will be able to complete an accurate report on Y.
- The team member will be able to set up Z in the system.
- Other

Provide Context

What's the "Why" of this training? Briefly explain why your department/ company completes the process this way, and the impact of this procedure, process, or action on the larger systems, processes, or organization. Help the new hire understand why this step/process/task/procedure is particularly important to the bigger picture, why the details must be included, the data must be accurate, the deadline met, the customer experience superior, and what happens next in the process.

The Content

This is where you detail what the new hire needs to do to achieve the outcomes you've listed above.

- Describe instructions step-by-step.
- Assume that they do not know what you might consider to be common knowledge.
- Spell out industry jargon and acronyms.
- Explain common questions and answers.
- Clarify where to find/whom to contact for additional information.
- Identify/Provide additional resources—examples, documents, hyperlinks, etc.

Sidenote: This is also an excellent opportunity to update or begin to create standard operating procedures around key processes and systems in your department—if you haven't already.

The specific schedule, topics, and measures of success are different for every job. But setting employees up to be competent members of and confident contributors to your team begins with creating a deliberate onboarding action plan for each new hire. Weave in the structured trainings over a period of time, such as 4 to 12 weeks or up to 12 months, depending on the position, and incorporate them alongside on-the-job experience that reinforces the training.

It won't be perfect, especially at first, but over time, ensuring that you and your new hire both understand what success looks like, and the new team member is equipped with the training and tools to thrive, will do wonders for your sanity, your new hire's success, and your team's productivity.

But don't stop there!

Spell Out S-U-C-C-E-S-S

Your new team member is off to a good start by getting trained in key systems and processes they need to be successful in their role, which is professional jet fuel for them and anxiety relief for you. But don't overlook the importance of clear expectations. In other words, what does "good" look like? If you assume they know, you will regret it.

From your perspective as their leader, what are you looking for in them? What are the signs, signals, and details that demonstrate your new team member is effectively performing their job duties well? Once again, the job description is the starting point—but only the starting point, because job descriptions commonly include vague language. Be prepared to explain what terms mean.

For example, *"Perform a thorough contract review for every project."* As the manager for the new hire, you should be able to define what "thorough" means and how "thorough" is measured. For example, *"The employee has ensured these specific areas are checked and confirmed for accuracy…"*

"Complete clear and detailed project reports." The manager should be able to define and show the new hire what *"clear and detailed project reports"* look like, how to create them, and where to find examples of them.

References to time, such as *"ASAP"* or *"delivered in a timely fashion,"* should be spelled out. Is that within one hour, twenty-four hours, a week, a month?

"Clearly communicate with the team." Sounds great! Now what does that actually mean? Is that a status report delivered once a month, a notation on the scrum board, or a thumbs-up emoji in the group chat?

"Provide superior service to every client." Yes! And just like those "5-star" reviews on Amazon, my idea of superior service and your idea of superior service don't always match up. So give examples of what superior service looks like in action.

Additionally:

- Explain how the employee's job performance will be measured.
- Ensure the employee is clear on their core responsibilities.
- Agree to regularly scheduled check-in meetings.
- Agree how you will communicate with one another—text, email, phone, Snapchat, Slack.
- Do you have an "open door" policy or is it more realistic for the employee to schedule time on your calendar to ensure your undivided attention?
- Explain what you need from them to build a strong working relationship.
- Ask them to spell out what they need from you to help them become a full contributing member of the team.

Establish Short-Term Objectives

Your new hire wants to feel useful immediately, but they are also learning and don't want to screw up. Make it safe for them to experiment

and explore. List a few activities, tasks, and responsibilities that the new team member should complete in the next couple of weeks, such as:

- Become familiar with commonly used software.
- Meet with specific team members in other departments and/or locations to better understand roles across the organization.
- Shadow other team members in the department.
- Meet with key stakeholders (clients, vendors, stakeholders, subcontractors, others whose relationships are essential to the individual's/ department's success.)
- Complete specific onboarding training modules.

Establish Midterm Objectives

Identify the top priorities that will define the employee's success in the next three to six months. It's important to evaluate what the department/organization needs and what the employee is (or thinks) they are ready for at this point. Consider how their onboarding training is preparing them to execute their job effectively. Your list will be different, but below are a few examples of possible midterm objectives:

- Effectively completes accounts payables process, ensuring that all documentation is submitted by deadline.
- Effectively determines scopes of work to ensure A, B, and C.
- Effectively analyzes contract requirements to confirm E, F, and G.
- Master billing processes.
- Deliver monthly reports to team.
- Seek quarterly feedback from project stakeholders.
- Secure three new clients.
- Complete training courses on a specific program.
- Establish working relationships with core department heads.

- Assess hiring needs for the next six months and prepare a written report.
- Successfully prepare two company newsletters.
- Develop and deliver a social marketing execution plan.
- Others based on the job description and demands of the role at this time.

Six-to-twelve-Month Goals:

Up to this point, your new team member's objectives have been focused on helping them learn the job and understand what success looks like in their role. And because you, your team, and others in the organization have done such a great job setting them up for success, they are likely itching to spread their wings.

Now it's time to look at what's possible from here and discuss goals for the next six to twelve months. You want to co-create the goal plan with them, not tell them what their goals are. Their input is key to *their* engagement in *their* goals. That said, your guidance is also essential.

As a start, I recommend goals in three general areas:

1. Department- or function-focused—This goal will likely be tied to your objectives as the leader of the department or area. It is important to the effective operation of the department and/or improves its operation.

2. Strategic-focused—This goal is linked to the organization's strategic plan. The team member can see how their role is connected to the bigger goals of the business.

3. Professional development—This goal emphasizes the importance of continuous learning and growth as a professional on your team, and moving toward mastery in key areas.

Once again, less is more. Solid goals have multiple steps, so keep the list to a few. The goals are the "what" will be accomplished. Your team member decides the "how"—how they will be accomplished. Keep in mind that these goals are a guide, and they may change. If department or organizational priorities change, individual goals may need to be adjusted as well.

Done well, goal conversations are energizing, exciting, and engaging. They give direction and focus, ensure that your team is moving toward a common vision or mission, connect the team member to the larger purpose of the organization, and they help to ensure results.

Key Points

When it comes to knowing what's expected of them, new hires need more than an offer letter and a welcome to the team. They need a clear job description, essential training, and concrete expectations. In other words, they must have a clear pathway to proficiency. It's essential that leaders:

- Ensure team members are trained to deliver on their responsibilities.
- Clearly explain what "success" looks like.
- Help new team members prioritize tasks.
- Define how their work will be measured—e.g., number of sales, accuracy rates, engaged clients, payments processed, etc.
- Guide them in setting exciting, impactful, and SMART goals (Specific, Measurable, Actionable, Relevant, and Timebound).

Once they've been successfully onboarded to your team, do not leave your employee stranded on Isolation Island. Your work as their leader/manager continues. It's critical that you are connecting and communicating regularly with them. Schedule time on your calendar to make sure that you're intentionally checking in and having regular structured conversations with them. We'll talk about connection and feedback in Chapters 4 and 9.

There Was a Will, but Not a Way

Will came to realize that his idea of being a leader, and the realities of the role, were light-years apart. While moving into leadership seemed like a great opportunity at the time, the demands were frustrating and unfulfilling. At this point in his career, his zone of genius is in connecting directly with clients. It's not only his passion, but it's also profitable for the organization.

Ultimately, after considerable soul-searching and a serious sit-down with his ego, he chose to return to his job as an individual performer, giving another manager the opportunity to step into Will's former role. That new leader is thriving—setting the team up for success and readily embracing the challenges. At some point, with a bit more experience and some leadership development training along the way, Will may want to explore a role in leadership in the future. For now, he's thriving.

Leadership isn't for everyone, and that's okay! It can be tremendously rewarding, but it is also incredibly demanding, with more responsibilities than most new leaders can begin to comprehend. And like new hires, new leaders also need to be set up to succeed.

CHAPTER 4

WAIT, WHAT? I HAVE TO TALK TO THEM?

Navigating the messy, difficult conversations

"If you don't risk anything, you risk even more."

— Erica Jong

L eadership can be a handsome suitor who will coax you into its embrace with the promise of opportunity, challenge, growth, and the chance to have a "real" impact.

Cassie is a good soldier in a large software company. When a key member of her team left the organization, Cassie saw an opportunity. Like most high achievers, Cassie couldn't resist the pull. She went to her leader and asked if she could restructure the department and move into the manager role. She had been in the department for seven years and was hungry to take on more responsibility.

Little did she realize when she went for the promotion to manager that the tables were turning. She was about to go from individual contributor as a corporate trainer to front-row student in the school of hard knocks.

As is often the case in the early days of a new leader romance, it's easy to disregard those little irritations that can distract you from the blissful ignorance of a good crush. In Cassie's case, the "little irritation" was the fact that she now had real, live employees reporting to her. Cassie's No. 1 concern in taking the position: navigating the messy people stuff, namely performance feedback.

Out of the gate, she hired a new member of the team, Liz. "I really liked her. I thought I could make her into the type of employee we needed in the department. I put up blinders. I needed her to be operating at a level she wasn't prepared to operate at. I work in training. I should be able to train her, right?" Or so Cassie told herself.

Like many leaders, Cassie is loyal, hardworking, empathetic and, yet, also like many leaders, she struggles to communicate expectations, provide feedback, and navigate challenging conversations, so that she can actually execute effectively as the manager and her team members can deliver the work successfully.

The issues started almost immediately as the training department's stakeholders began reporting their concerns about Liz to Cassie. But she kept hoping things would get better. Cassie was employing the very same avoidance strategies that she'd seen countless times before in the leaders she trains. The situation was made even more painful for Cassie because her job as a trainer was to help other leaders in the organization navigate precisely these types of challenges. "If anyone knew better, I did. But I buried it. I did Liz no favors. By the time I had 'the conversation' with her, it was terrible."

For Cassie, being "liked" kept her safe and seemingly far from the perils of the leadership ledge. Even though, intellectually, she knew that she needed to engage in difficult conversations with Liz, the idea of delivering constructive criticism caused her waves of anxiety, leaving her paralyzed. "I knew I needed to give her feedback early and often. But I was scared

that maybe she wouldn't like me anymore. It was selfish. I was driven by the desire to avoid my own discomfort. If I had shared the issues upfront and said, 'Let's work through it,' maybe the outcome would have been different."

Often leaders, especially newer leaders, second-guess themselves and their instincts. They fear they will come across as "micromanaging" or "nitpicking," so they look the other way, promise themselves that if "it happens again," they will address it, and then they don't, for whatever reason. The conversations only get harder because, with each infraction, the frustration grows, and so, too, do the stakes, as well as the stories.

Many studies have focused on the significant struggle leaders—both new and experienced—face in stepping up to difficult conversations, and I've seen it time and again in working with leaders and teams. It's a huge derailer. After all, work gets done through conversation, and conversations can't all be feel-good happy talk. Moreover, most team members want to know how they are doing and what they can do to be more effective, as well as what they are doing that's working well.

Leaders who withhold essential performance feedback for fear of not being liked or hurting the other's feelings are merely engaging in an indirect form of cruelty. The only person you're trying to protect is yourself. The employee's livelihood is dependent upon their ability to perform their job duties up to the established business standards. To not tell the team member where they are performing well AND where they need to develop/improve their skills is undermining that employee's ability to step up to the plate. You're hobbling their growth, not protecting them from temporary discomfort.

Team members don't come to work—in most cases—intentionally trying to underperform. Quite the opposite. They want to do well. It's up to you, as their leader, to shine a light on the rocks they are tripping over and help them devise a strategy to remove them or work around them.

For Cassie, it was being a dedicated and effective team member, as well as being liked, that earned her the leadership position in the first place. It was important to her that her team like her. But it was also important that her stakeholders not only like her, but respect what she and her team delivered.

It is a powerful lesson for leaders: address the issues and concerns promptly, as well as deliver accolades and congratulations regularly. It is through both that you are intentionally creating a dialogue-rich environment in which you are regularly discussing what's working well and what isn't. As the leader, your actions define the team culture, and that includes creating a culture of communication.

Step Up to That Difficult Conversation Using Compassionate Candor

When your role demands that you stand toe-to-toe with a difficult conversation, it's important to have a plan. Here's a step-by-step approach you can experiment with. Use this as a guide, not a prescription.

Step 1: Navigate the Emotional Vortex

When we, as leaders, become frustrated with our teammates, it's very easy to be sucked into the emotional vortex of the situation. From that place, we can't see, think, or act clearly. Here, the emotions are driving the bus—usually straight off a cliff.

For example, we may get triggered by a team member's strong personality, so we may react from a place of anger-fueled judgment and "should-ing" all over them. They "shouldn't be so aggressive." They "shouldn't interrupt." They "should be a more respectful team player."

When the emotions are running hot, the "shoulds" are everywhere, and we are more likely to step right smack into them. Been there; done that.

Unless the building is burning down or the employee has put themselves or others in danger, do not have the conversation when volatile emotions are spiking. You know the ones—anger, hurt, frustration, shame—the emotions that make you want to throw something, curse at the other person, or engage in other unhelpful and unproductive behaviors.

Rather, pause, observe your reactions, and get curious. Be a scientist. It's often noted among psychologists and human behavior experts that it can be very helpful to name the emotions and the physical reactions you're experiencing. For example: "I feel anger. I notice that my jaw is clenching. My throat is tight. My heart is racing. My face feels hot."

Making this simple shift in how you acknowledge your feelings also helps you to have the emotions rather than the emotions having you. To bring that point home further, I find it is helpful for my clients to draw a stick figure that represents them, and a line looping around the stick figure (see illustration—and don't judge me for my lack of Canva skills). This represents the rope of emotions. When the emotions have you, it can feel like a rope is wrapped tightly around you. You try to move, but the rope just tightens further. List the emotions that have you now. What do they feel like?

Next, give yourself a break. Take a walk, preferably outside. Listen to some calming music. Do a five-minute meditation. Get a cup of coffee. Work on something else for a while. Go for a run. Hop on your Peloton. Watch videos of puppies. Whatever you need to do, just pause and get away from the situation so you can reset. Do NOT address the issue until you are grounded, and, most importantly, you have a PLAN of action.

After the break, draw the stick figure again. This time, you, the stick figure, are holding the rope of emotions. The emotions don't have you trapped in their unyielding grip, rather you have them. Identify a few helpful emotions that you want to put into action as you navigate your next steps. For example, compassion, empathy, courage, respect, curiosity, etc. Now you get to decide how you will use those emotions.

Step 2: Get Clear on Your Motives

"The road to hell is paved with good intentions…" What are yours?

Honestly answer this question: "What is my motivation, my intention?" It's a tougher question than it seems, particularly when you put a spotlight on the emotions that are driving that intention. Consider these follow-up questions: "Do I really want to win? Control? Punish? Prove I'm right? Avoid the bigger problem? Shame the other person?"

If you're going into the conversation seeking to win, control, shame, or punish, it will likely backfire. These are motives that come from a place of judgment. And, I promise you, the other person knows when you're judging them. Their "spidey sense" is remarkably acute.

Or is your intention to help this person succeed? Move the department goals further along? Support them as a team member? Create a culture of mutual respect? When your actions are rooted in proactive, rather than reactive motives, they provide a foundation that increases the likelihood you'll be able to successfully navigate difficult conversations.

Step 3: Show Up as the Leader You Would Want to Work For

I encourage my clients to use what I refer to as the "I Am" exercise. This enables you to be intentional about applying both your personal/professional values and what your organization needs from you as a leader in the challenging moment.

First, what's your QVC? (Admittedly shopping is never far from my mind, and QVC used to be—maybe it still is—a home shopping channel.) But for these purposes, QVC is the list of qualities, values, and characteristics you can bring when addressing the challenging situation. These might also be your strengths and ninja skills.

Take a minute and write down four or five qualities, values, and characteristics that represent what is most important to you as a leader. For example, Calm, Compassionate, Courageous, Positive, Organized, Respectful, Resourceful, Action-driven, Detail-oriented, etc.

Next, consider what your position in the organization needs from you. Make a list. This might be Creative Thinker, Problem-Solver, Leader, Subject Matter Expert, Detail Diva, Strategic Visionary, Administrative Guru, etc. This is the expertise, knowledge, and wisdom that are essential in your role. Again, make a list of the four or five items that are most important in your role.

Third, create your Anchor Statement. This is the "I Am" statement that captures the essence of the two lists you've created. It enables you to focus on what you are fully capable of bringing to the challenging situation. It starts with the words "I am" and it sums up who you are when you are at your most confident, fully effective self. For example, "I am a calm, resourceful problem-solver." Keep it short and to the point. The two lists are your inspiration. You want to capture the essence of them, not every word you've written.

As your anchor, the "I Am" statement helps keep you from heading off course when situations become challenging. It reminds you of who you are at your best, at your core. Look at it before you walk into what may be a challenging meeting. Call it to mind when talking with a difficult coworker, when addressing a controversial situation, and when providing necessary feedback to your team member.

Put your anchor statement in multiple places where you can see it several times a day. Memorize it and make it your mantra for the professional, the person, the leader, the teammate you are fully capable of being, even in the most challenging situations.

Step 4: Pluck the BRR

My little dogs, Cooper and Cash, love to go to the park and run and chase squirrels. They are likely convinced that if I would just give them a little more lead on the leash, or if I would run faster, they would catch one of those critters. It is their purest form of joy, until the prickly burrs start sticking to their fur. They look at me with that pained expression, eyes pleading for me to do something. I figure it must feel like doggie diaper rash. And I have no choice but to wrestle those spiky sharp things out of their fur—and fast.

The same is true for your difficult conversations. Like those sticky burrs, the first infraction that you notice is slightly painful and a little annoying, but maybe, if you ignore it, it will work its way out. Then the behavior occurs a few more times. And just like a few more burrs attached to the leg of your pants or tangled in your dog's fur, there's no more ignoring the situation because that little annoyance has morphed into a particularly painful scenario. Now you, dear leader, have a situation that needs to be addressed. The burr—or BRR in this case—needs to be plucked.

Consider the following:

> B—What's the **Behavior** you are observing that needs to be addressed?
>
> R—Is it **Recurring** and not an isolated incident?
>
> R—What is the **Risk** to the project, the team, the culture, the client, or other if this behavior continues?

Get clear on the behavior or situation that you need to address. For example, team member Ian, who is relatively new to the department, is interrupting and speaking over others in meetings. Consider if this is an isolated incident or a recurring **Behavior.** You decide that this appears to be a **Recurring** behavior; it has occurred during the past three team meetings. You also observe that other team members are not participating as actively. You conclude that the **Risk** of Ian's behavior is that it is diminishing his teammates' engagement in essential discussions.

What's important here is that you are focusing on what actually occurred in the meeting—what you have seen and heard. The facts. Treat the facts as you would if you were reporting the weather. "It's 28 degrees, cloudy, and winds are 5 mph from the north." The facts are neutral. They are neither good nor bad, they are merely what has or is occurring.

It's essential that you quell your urge to craft imaginary emotion-triggering scenarios. These are the nasty stories, hurtful assumptions, and sweeping conclusions that we draw from our negative interpretations of the facts. They quickly have us tripping over the leadership ledge and landing hard on the sharp edges of our false deductions. Our quickly crafted imaginary scenarios cause strong emotions to ramp up, while simultaneously paralyzing us from effective action, or worse, propelling us to destructive action. They are not helpful, and indulging them can cause significant damage to leadership effectiveness and team relationships. Truth be told—we've all indulged them and then wished that we hadn't. In other words, the stories we tell ourselves about others and their motivations are often wrong and usually cause pain.

For example: Ian, as you've observed, is frequently interrupting and speaking over others in meetings. An imaginary scenario starts to take shape in your mind. You quietly paint a picture of Ian as "an arrogant and disrespectful jerk, who thinks he knows it all." His behavior reminds you of a controlling boss you once worked for. This triggers anger and resentment, and pours emotional gasoline on an otherwise pretty banal situation. This emotionally charged reaction then has you teetering between the either/or of unhelpful options:

- Either "I'm going to give Ian a piece of mind and tell him to shut his mouth."
- Or "I'll just wait and see how this plays out because if I say anything to Ian, he'll probably accuse me of playing favorites or question my authority or both."

Neither the imaginary scenario nor the responses are helpful. Rather, they have you reacting harshly or protecting yourself. Both are a distraction from the bigger issue: the impact of Ian's behavior on the team's effectiveness and ability to make progress toward the team's goals.

Reset by painting a different picture in your mind:

Ian is enthusiastic about his perspectives. His way of connecting with others is by talking. He doesn't realize that he's interrupting and speaking over others; he thinks he's engaging with the group. He doesn't recognize the impact that his behavior is having on others because it's a blind spot for him, not an intentional affront to his teammates. Like other members of the team, Ian's sincere desire is to be a helpful and effective teammate.

Step 5: Ask Questions and You Shall Receive Answers

In an ideal situation, the team has established in its team pact how team members will work most effectively together, including engaging in dialogue and disagreement (see Chapter 6). But until the team establishes its pact, addressing issues that arise on the team often defaults to the leader. Lucky you.

In this case, as we've discussed, you've recognized and separated from unhelpful emotions. You are clear on your motives—you want to help set Ian up for success. You've defined your "I Am" statement, such as, "I am a courageous, generous, and solution-oriented leader."

Now, share your observations of what you've noticed in the meetings with Ian, and ask him to share his perspective of the situation. For example:

"Ian, I know you are new to the team and want to make a positive impression. I appreciate your enthusiasm, and I sincerely want to help you build good relationships with your teammates." (Motivation)

"I've noticed in the past three staff meetings that you've interrupted or talked over teammates in making your points. In today's meeting, I observed that you were doing most of the talking, and team members were engaging less and less as the meeting went on. At times, I realized that even I was hesitant to challenge you on your points." (Stating what you've personally seen, heard, and experienced.)

"How do you see your interactions with the team?" (Inviting dialogue)

The human brain is wired to be scanning for danger constantly. So, Ian may, in fact, initially shut down or become defensive and react with something like, "Well that's their problem if they can't make their point or they're too afraid to speak up."

In that case, reset and restate. You may be emotionally triggered by Ian's reaction. Reset mentally with your "I Am" anchor statement and restate your motivation. "Ian, I sincerely want to help you build strong relationships with the team, and I want to encourage everyone's input in advancing the team's goals." This helps neutralize the dialogue to restore psychological safety with Ian, reduce his threat response, and restate your overarching intention.

Invite him back to the dialogue. "Can we both agree that tapping into the intelligence and perspectives from the group helps create a more effective and inclusive team culture?" This helps establish shared understanding on a point that is important to both you and the team as a whole.

Next encourage Ian to identify the solution. "How might you approach our next team meeting in a way that encourages discussion among everyone in the group, including you?" Asking a solution-oriented question puts Ian in charge of his response.

Sure, as the boss, you could tell Ian what to do: "In the next meeting, you need to talk less." But just because you can doesn't mean you should. Consider what you want as a leader in the bigger picture. Ian is a valuable member of the team who can learn and grow in his interpersonal relationships. Telling him what to do is more likely to shame him and cause an unnecessary rift in your relationship, and ignoring his behavior is harmful to both Ian and the team. Those burrs just compound and get stickier and pricklier by the day.

It's more likely that Ian is truly trying to enthusiastically engage with his teammates and doesn't realize that his exuberance is causing others to shut down. Once a light is shined on this blind spot, it's quite possible that, while Ian may be initially embarrassed and possibly defensive, he will welcome the opportunity to connect more effectively with his team members.

Ongoing Dialogue Fuels a Culture of Compassionate Candor

As for Cassie, she took to heart the difficult lesson she learned in her experience with Liz, who left after less than a year. "Sarah was hired to replace Liz, and I was not going to make the same mistake again. We meet weekly, and we discuss what's going well, what challenges we are experiencing, what our stakeholders need, and how we are responding to those needs. It's an environment of ongoing conversation and feedback, both ways. I'm seeking feedback from her as much as I'm delivering feedback."

Create an environment for ongoing dialogue. Establish regular check-in meetings with your team members. The discussion areas listed below can be used as a guide or inspiration for your own list of topics and questions. The key is to ensure that the meetings have an intentional focus.

Team Member's Discussion Areas

1. These are some of the strengths and skills I'm leaning into.
2. This is an area that is going well for me (or this is a win that I'm proud of).
3. These are strengths and skills that I'm noticing I need help developing.
4. This is an area that I'm struggling with or finding challenging.
5. It would be helpful to me as a team member if I had more/less of this from my leader.
6. What does the leader need more of/less of from me?

Team Leader's Discussion Areas

1. These are some of the strengths and skills I'm observing in the team member.
2. This is an area that I've observed is going well for the team member (or a win/accomplishment that I've observed).
3. I've observed the team member struggling or challenged by this.
4. What does the team member need more of/less of from me, their leader?
5. As the leader, I need more of/less of this from the team member.

Difficult discussions only become more challenging when we avoid them. Admittedly, having a strategy and a plan to address them more effectively won't magically make them fun or even easy. They are still difficult conversations. However, preparing and taking a constructive and intentionally proactive approach will significantly increase the likelihood that they are more successful and less stressful.

Choose to create an environment of ongoing conversation across your team. Work with team members to establish guidelines for how everyone in the department will address breakdowns in communication, unmet expectations, frustrations, disappointment, and anger with one another. While you are their leader, you are not their referee. But as their leader, it is up to you to help them grow and become more effective, contributing members of your team and the organization, and that means effectively walking the leadership ledge that is the difficult conversation.

CHAPTER 5

COIN TOSS: KILL THE TEAM OR FIRE MYSELF? ALIGN THEM INSTEAD (PART I)

"To handle yourself, use your head; to handle others, use your heart."

—Eleanor Roosevelt

The group gathered around the table. There were ten of them assigned to this multimillion-dollar project. None of them had worked together before, and the project leader, Christopher, had only been with the company for six months. Never before had he been responsible for a project of this size or significance.

Taxpayer-funded, it was the largest project of its type that the small company had undertaken in its history. It was an extremely high-profile endeavor, in which all eyes would be on the project team's results. It would be closely scrutinized by the media, politicians, and influencers in the community. The stakes were huge.

If this job went well, there likely would be several more to follow. It had the potential to dramatically impact not just the business, but also the community for generations to come. If it went poorly, the effect could be crippling for the organization's reputation, and, most definitely, its bottom line.

Christopher is a six-foot-five-inch former Marine with a deadly serious demeanor and a brilliant smile that rarely slips across his face. He was prepared to do everything he could to ensure the mission's success. But most importantly, he was committed to being the most effective leader he could be. For months leading up to this project, he had worked with a leadership development coach to develop his leadership competencies, identify how he got in his own way, what he could do about it, and get clarity on his own leadership values and philosophy.

Hero Leader

Christopher had come from a company that prized individualism and the fantasy of the "hero leader." It was stuck in the twentieth-century command-and-control culture, in which the terms "I don't know," "collaboration," or "collective intelligence" would have you enduring mocking stares, labored sighs, and rolling eyes. He hated it. He saw the destructive impact that the climate of competition and "win at any cost" had on morale and employee retention. It was a place where the boss was in charge and was there to control. The staff were the hired help. They were there to work in service to the "cha-ching" of the bottom line. They'd better not screw up.

Yet, as much as Christopher disliked the culture of his previous company, he'd also done very well there and was used to being among the keepers of knowledge, the answer man, and one of the key "go-to guys" when work needed to get done. His projects were smaller, the stakes were lower, and he knew enough that he could bluff his way through if questioned. While he didn't believe it was a sustainable environment over the long term, for the time that Christopher was there, it fueled his confidence, as well as his desire for more challenge and professional growth.

Be careful what you wish for. At Christopher's new company, with its big projects and continuous learning philosophy, the culture was one of collaboration. But the leaders were also managers, and Christopher was managing this massive project with hundreds of moving parts and substantial complexities, as well as leading and trying to develop his team.

He recognized early on that, at this company, the leaders were held to high expectations. In fact, it was part of what attracted him to the organization. They were to deliver with excellence for the client, and do so while working in service to their teams. Most of the managers were leading multiple teams at the same time. They were to clear the roadblocks that would get in the way, and roadblocks always got in the way. The project manager/leaders were expected to take ownership, help one another learn from mistakes, and create a psychologically safe environment where errors could be caught early and addressed.

That said, this company, with established core systems, good intentions that were usually backed up with actions, and a strong track record of success, was like many small businesses of its type. It fell into a common trap. A group of people were regularly thrown together and told that they were now a "team." They might work together for twelve to thirty-six months, and then the individuals will be reassigned to other projects where they were again expected to become a "team."

Noble Desires

Christopher knew he had to scale his capacity. A project of this size and complexity required him to rely on the expertise, knowledge, and commitment of those around him. He had to do everything he could to create the conditions for success on this project. And that required he build a culture in which a group of people who'd been tossed together could function effectively as a team—and quickly. They didn't have six months to figure one another out.

Christopher was intrinsically motivated. He genuinely wanted to help those around him grow as professionals, leaders, and become both more effective team members and thriving human beings. He sought to be a leader who was valued, respected, and appreciated for what his team could together achieve. Noble desires, indeed. He was also, like virtually every high-performing leader I've worked with, utterly terrified of failure.

He stood at the base of the proverbial mountain. Wanting a high-performing, flourishing, and successful team is the easy part. Creating it—climbing that mountain—requires a massive commitment—from everyone—not just the leader.

Christopher was determined to set up his team for success coming out of the gate. He knew there would be multiple variables, frustrations, and many, many unforeseen circumstances and setbacks that would arise over the next thirty-six months. Whatever he could do to align the team and establish clarity, commitment, and communication, up front, he would.

He also was acutely tuned in to "WIIFM" (what's in it for me). The success of this team would have a profound and powerful impact on Christopher's reputation as a leader and his future opportunities.

Your team members are your most important stakeholders. The only way to achieve your department's or organization's projects, or your own objectives, is through them. Ignore them, disregard them, minimize them at your peril. Yet few team leaders and team members truly understand how to create a team culture and environment in which they can navigate stress, frustration, conflict, and dysfunction, and work most effectively together.

GO T-E-A-M!

In many organizations, there is an assumption when it comes to teams that if you've been on a team—you know, softball, soccer, football; if you've watched a team—Superbowl, World Cup, World Series; if you can spell the word T-E-A-M, well, by golly, you should just know how to be a team! And if you make reference to the Tuckman Model, you're nothing short of a team genius! Surely, you've seen the poster TEAMWORK, with everyone rowing in the same direction. Now, GO!

There are several fuzzy pixels in this seemingly perfect team picture. For starters, creating, developing, and sustaining an effective team is, indeed, work. And, I don't say that lightly. You will encounter challenges, unexpected situations, difficult team dynamics, and quite possibly—even likely—crises. And while there is no foolproof formula to ensure that every team you lead or participate in is like that idyllic image of rowing along on the calm, glassy pristine waters, you can create a team infrastructure and environment that will be far better equipped to withstand the difficult and challenging choppy surf with more ease and less stress.

There are three key components to your team infrastructure: 1. Your Why—Your purpose for being a team. 2. Your What—What you are together responsible for creating, delivering, executing. 3. Your How—How you are going to work most effectively together to achieve your "What" and fulfill your "Why."

These form the foundation for your team pact. I use the word "pact" because the word's root is "peace." It's not merely an agreement, a charter, or a contract; it is a pact. It is your commitment to the project, your team members, and the organization. It spells out how you, together, will ensure that you've articulated not just what <u>you will do</u>—your roles and responsibilities—but how <u>you will be</u>—your behavior—along the way.

Disrespect, Dysfunction, and the Catastrophic Culture

In the winter of 1986, I was putting myself through college, working in the newsroom at an NPR-affiliated public radio station. On the morning of January 28, the cold air was brisk with anticipation and excitement. After months of hype and several delays, the space shuttle *Challenger* would lift off with a crew of seven, including Christa McAuliffe. Christa, a civilian, was to be the first teacher in space. Classrooms around the country had wheeled in television sets so that students could watch the launch live. Christa's parents, Edward and Grace Corrigan, stood in the stands at Cape Canaveral to watch their daughter soar into history.

As all of us who were around on that tragic day remember that seventy-three seconds after takeoff, the shuttle exploded, killing the crew. When I had to break into regularly scheduled programming to report the tragedy, I strained to keep my voice even as tears filled my eyes and my heart broke for those lost. To this day, a lump still rises in my throat when I think about that morning.

Investigations would reveal that, from a technical standpoint, the O-ring on the rocket boosters failed due to the unusually cold temperatures. Upon the tenth anniversary of the tragedy, in 1996, Columbia University sociologist Diane Vaughan released the book *The Challenger Launch Decision. Risky Technology, Culture, and Deviance at NASA*, which revealed a "normalization of deviance" within the space agency.

In a later interview with Consulting News Line, she explained, *"If there are problems, the tendency of corporate or public agency administrators is to blame individuals. However, organization characteristics—cultures, structures, politics, economic resources, their presence or absence, their allocation—put pressure on individuals to behave in deviant ways to achieve organization goals."*[11] In other words, the pressures of the culture will compromise established processes and procedures.

Seventeen years later, the space shuttle *Columbia* would break apart upon re-entry, once again killing all seven astronauts onboard. The agency's culture was a key contributor, along with politics, budgets, and managerial complacency.

---

[11] Consultant, May 2008, Interview : Diane Vaughan Sociologist, Columbia University https://www.consultingnewsline.com/Info/Vie%20du%20Conseil/Le%20Consultant%20du%20mois/Diane%20Vaughan%20(English).html

The series of catastrophic events involving the Boeing 737 Max, the aircraft's failed safety audits, and the allegations of safety issues involving the 787 point to a more recent example of the potential devastation that can stem from a dysfunctional or toxic corporate culture.

Each of these examples, while complex and multifaceted in the layers that led to failure, all felt the powerful and tragic impact of toxic cultures. In their report *"An Empirical Study Analyzing Job Productivity in Toxic Workplace Environments,"*[12] the authors note, "Studies have shown that 80 percent of the issues and concerns regarding employees' productivity are related to the type of work environment in which they operationalize their assigned tasks."

Put simply, 80 percent of the problems, issues, and inefficiencies a team experiences are directly related to the culture or environment of the team. Twenty percent of the problems are related to the tasks to be completed.

Friction, Confusion, and Underperformance

Organizational and project teams are commonly given a multitude of seemingly contradictory messages: "stay on budget," "create a fantastic client experience," "build trust," "make a profit," "be empathetic," "stay on schedule," "engage in healthy conflict," "hold people accountable," "execute with excellence," "follow processes," "innovate," "engage the team," "take charge," "do it right," and the list goes on.

The "team members," particularly in smaller organizations, come together and proceed to try to "get things done," "take action," "get after it." They may all be moving, but it's usually in different directions. Why? Because virtually no effort has been made to align them as a team and gain clarity around why they have been brought together, what they are to achieve

---

[12] Anjum A, Ming X, Siddiqi AF, Rasool SF. An Empirical Study Analyzing Job Productivity in Toxic Workplace Environments. Int J Environ Res Public Health. 2018 May 21;15(5):1035. doi: 10.3390/ijerph15051035. PMID: 29883424; PMCID: PMC5982074.

specifically as a team, and exactly how they are to work most effectively (behave) as a team.

Left to its own devices, your team's culture will emerge organically for better or worse. Even if you have a group of "really great, smart people," that is no guarantee the dynamic will manifest in a "really great smart team." It's imperative to the success of the project, the initiative, the team, and the organization that team leaders and team members together intentionally create a culture that enables the group to work effectively, navigate conflict, and move in concert toward the desired goal.

To paraphrase these words commonly attributed to Peter Drucker, management consultant, author, and educator, "Only three things happen naturally in organizations [teams]: friction, confusion, and underperformance. Everything else requires leadership."

You've likely been on more than your fair share of well-meaning and well-intentioned intact teams and project teams that floundered, if not failed. After all, according to the 2020 Standish Group's CHAOS report, nearly 70 percent of projects fail. According to Gallup, "Projects often fail because organizations put more emphasis on rational factors than on employees' psychological engagement—and the cost to organizations is enormous."

Simply put, too few teams discuss HOW they will work effectively together, let alone build a team infrastructure to ensure that the culture they create is conducive to the success of the project, as well as the success of the individual team members.

Some teams may agree to a few ground rules or norms, such as, "We are trustworthy, respectful, and accountable to one another." But they don't discuss what trustworthy, respectful, and accountable actually looks like in action on this team and in the context of this particular project in this particular organization.

Then someone drops the ball on an important deliverable. And the ugly imaginary scenarios and stories start to swirl. *"That person can't ever be trusted. They don't care about the company."* The situation is compounded when the issue isn't discussed to better understand the why behind the breakdown. And more emotional fuel is poured onto the smoldering flames of discontent, as assumptions are made, and fingers are pointed.

It's likely that we've all experienced the psychological and financial toll of ineffective, disengaged, and toxic teams. The natural next question is, *How do I actually create an effective team culture that isn't mired in friction, confusion, and underperformance?*

In my work with small business teams, we walk through a series of steps inspired by Organizational Relationship Systems Coaching, Systemic Team Coaching, and the work of the Gottman Institute, which enable the team to develop their team pact.

A Pact for Peace … Respect and Trust

Teams that have greater respect, trust, communication, and accountability experience greater peace. They also demonstrate a stronger commitment to the project and to one another. They create a culture far better equipped to deliver effectively on the "what."

The process of creating the Team Alignment Pact is designed to achieve **three key objectives**:

1. Enable the team to discuss and determine their core purpose/their "why" as a team.

2. Enable the team to articulate in the team pact the culture they will create and the shared expectations for how they will behave and interact as a team to create that culture.

3. Shine a light on the ways in which team members can slip into dysfunction, and how they will support one another in moving through and past the dysfunctional behaviors that negatively impact/derail the team.

Back to Christopher. He was acutely aware that he and his team would face relentless pressure and multiple challenges throughout the project. He needed to align them. They needed to be one team working toward a common goal, not a collection of individuals with ego-centric personal agendas.

With the help of a team coach, the project team created their team pact. It wouldn't guarantee that there wouldn't be challenges and setbacks, but it would ensure that the team had a plan for how they would work most effectively together—especially when things got difficult, because things always get difficult! That was simply the nature of the industry in which Christopher and his team worked.

Through a series of three team alignment sessions and team coaching, the members established their team pact. They defined the team's "why," a clear purpose for their work. They communicated what they needed and expected from one another as individuals and as a team. They articulated what success looked like and how they would work effectively together to achieve that success. They established the parameters for how they would address the conflict and dysfunction that would inevitably emerge.

Over several months, the team continued to revisit the pact, as well as integrate other tools around psychological safety and stakeholder communication. The pact and the ongoing conversations around team effectiveness provided a framework to address the inescapable challenges and conflicts that arose. The clearly articulated expectations and understanding around not just what would be done on this project, but also how the team members would behave, helped ensure that the race to the finish, while it wasn't easy, it was easier and less stressful, with less dysfunction and little-to-no toxicity.

The process required Christopher to step into his role as leader in a way that was very different from how he had led in the past. He needed to engage his team throughout the project. In effect he needed to lead from three positions: In some cases, he needed to be the leader in front—clearing the path and leading the charge. In others, he needed to be the leader beside, standing alongside his team, acting as a fellow team member and co-creator. And in others, he needed to be the leader behind, creating opportunities for others to step up, to grow, and to develop as leaders themselves.

The project became a model for the organization, and Christopher went on to secure a significant promotion in which he would impact multiple project teams.

How did he do it? In Chapter 6, I'll give you the steps, tools, and strategy to begin to create a Team Alignment Pact that provides the framework to create a successful team culture, *if you're willing to take the necessary action.*

COIN TOSS: KILL THE TEAM OR FIRE MYSELF? ALIGN THEM INSTEAD (PART II)

"I am a member of a team, and I rely on the team; I defer to it and sacrifice for it, because the team, not the individual, is the ultimate champion."

—Mia Hamm,
two-time Women's World Cup Champion

In Part I (Chapter 5), I shared Christopher's story about his efforts to create a high-functioning team that could deliver on an extraordinarily high-stakes project. In this chapter, Part II, I'll walk you through the "why" and the "how" to help you establish your own high-performance team.

At the core of a high performance team is what I refer to as the team alignment pact. I use the word "pact" because at the word's root is "peace." Creating and upholding the team pact, which articulates the team's core purpose, the team culture, and steps to address dysfunction, requires commitment, engagement from all team members, and a willingness to keep the agreement both dynamic and front and center throughout the life of the team.

The development of the team pact is the first step in helping the team to create a framework for how its members will work most effectively together in service to the team's purpose and the organization's larger goals.

Step 1—Define Your Why: The Team's Purpose

What's your team's "Why"? Why has this team been established? Why is this team uniquely qualified to deliver the desired outcome? Your "Why" is the objective or purpose of the team. It serves as the compass when dysfunction arises—and it will—sure as the buffalo gnats will be biting in the spring. The team's why or purpose statement helps the team members to reorient and return to their fundamental reason for being when they are pulled off course.

With your team, use the straightforward questions below to help you define your team's purpose. Do NOT complete this in isolation, and hand it over to your team for them to admire your fine work and gasp in awe at your sheer brilliance. The first step in building a high-functioning team is engaging them in the co-creation of the Team Alignment Pact.

Defining Your "Why" (Intact Team)

The questions below can be used for any intact team, but for example, let's assume that yours is the accounting team.

1. What impact does your organization/company have on your community?
2. What knowledge, skills, gifts do the members of this team (e.g. accounting team) bring to achieving this impact?
3. Why is the accounting team's role important to the organization, other departments, clients, others?
4. What is most important about this role?

     a. What else is important?

     b. And what else?

5. What is the larger mission/purpose that the accounting team serves?

When coaching a team through this process, I break this exercise down and ask the team members to discuss their answers to each of the five questions and capture key points on flip chart paper or digital whiteboards. From there, group members are asked to select key words from the discussion that should serve as inspiration and/or essential points they believe should be part of the purpose statement.

Using the inspiration words selected by the team members, each person or small group—depending on the number of people in the session—are invited to write a draft statement that captures the (accounting) team's "Why." Then the full group discusses the most important or resonant elements from the draft purpose statements. Working through a couple iterations, the group will together decide on its final team purpose statement.

Please note that this should be a statement—no more than two sentences—not a dissertation. It's succinct and impactful. And, most importantly, it reflects the themes that emerged from the discussion with the entire group—not just the points from a couple of people.

A similar process is used for project teams, but, in this case, the client is the primary focus of the questions.

Defining Your "Why" (Project Team)

1. Who is the key client on this project?

2. Why is this project important to the client?

3. What's most important to them?

4. And what else is important to them?

5. What is the client's larger mission/purpose that this project serves?

6. Consider the client's impact on the community, the client's goals, values, budget, timelines, etc.

   a. Avoid the urge to oversimplify this or rubberstamp it: "They want a cool website." "They want their warehouse built." "They want the new equipment to work." "They want a functioning software program." You get the idea. It's easy to come up with a trite simple statement like those above, but that undermines the "why" of this exercise.

   b. Articulating what's truly most important to the client, as the team sees it, creates a dialogue around the bigger picture, the greater good, and the deeper meaning of the work the team is going to do. That dialogue creates a more potent connection to the client and to the community the client serves.

   c. Put yourselves in the client's/stakeholders' shoes and consider what else might be important to them and their larger mission.

7. What are other big-picture perspectives about the client that should be kept top of mind? These are key considerations that are important for the project team to know when preparing to work together in the months ahead.

The team purpose exercise is an excellent way to enable the team members to connect to both the client's and the organization's larger mission, and it is a powerful means of helping team members bond with one another. Through the process of co-creation, the group acknowledges the value each person brings to the project. Moreover, team members are learning to effectively articulate what is important about this project.

In some cases, it can be useful when aligning the team to hold off on the purpose discussion until after the group has had time to discuss the type of environment or culture they do and don't want to create. However, depending on the nature of the team, the purpose exercise allows the team to think in concrete terms about what they are there to create together. This focus on the "doing" can then help the team feel more comfortable discussing the "being" — how they are going to behave as team members.

You've defined your "Why." Now let's look at the "How." How will you ensure that you work effectively together to deliver on your team's purpose? The "How" requires a careful examination of the "being" and the "doing" of both leadership and teamwork.

Step 2—Address the Herd of Elephants in the Room: Drama, Discomfort & Distress

(The following steps are geared toward project teams, but they can be easily modified for intact teams.)

The Post-it Notes covered the walls. "Backstabbing" "Frustration" "Lack of trust" "No accountability" "Stress" "Poor communication" "Disrespect" "Conflict" "Gossip" "Mind games" "Negativity" "Contempt" "Finger-pointing" "Toxicity" "Failure"

The group of newly assembled team members was answering the question *"What behaviors do you see on a 'team' when the culture is dysfunctional or even toxic?"*

They had come together to "align"—to determine how exactly they were going to work as a team. The first exercise of the day in the team alignment workshop was to help each of the team members share their ideas about what a dysfunctional team looks like.

From there, the individuals gave examples of what the words on the Post-it Notes looked like to them in action. "Poor communication to me means the project manager is making decisions about the deliverables without talking to me about how those decisions are going to impact the overall timeline," one team member said. "It means I'm not copied on emails about project changes," another team member said.

The first step in addressing team dysfunction is to get clarity about what it looks like and feels like to the participants. Follow the steps below to structure the discussion.

The exercise:

1. Give each person a stack of Post-it Notes and a black marker.

2. Pose this question to the group: **"What behaviors do you see on a 'team' when the culture is dysfunctional or even toxic?"**

3. This is a rapid-fire exercise. Allow about sixty to ninety seconds for each person to individually come up with as many answers as possible. Encourage them to write one idea per Post-it, and keep each to just a couple of words.

4. Next, ask each person to pick out their top five dysfunctional behaviors from their Post-it Notes and place them up on a flip chart, whiteboard, or electronic whiteboard, and share examples of what the dysfunctional behavior looks like, sounds like, and feels like in action.

5. Finally, discuss what the team notices. Are there common themes emerging? If two people listed the same items, ask each to explain how they experience that behavior. For example, if two people or more write the word "distrust," ask them to explain what distrust looks like to them. What are the actions, words, behaviors of distrust?

This exercise helps the team see from the start how each person may interpret behaviors differently. What is poor communication to one person may be seen as disrespect by another, but unless the team starts with an open dialogue about the issues that are likely to cause conflict and dysfunction, the group will spend months trying to figure one another out. The behaviors that set off Tulsi, trigger Ryan, and send Amber retreating into silence are likely to be very different.

This is also the time for team members to acknowledge some of their own dysfunctional tendencies.

Step 3—Acknowledge the Four Horsemen of Destructive Communication

Criticism. Contempt. Defensiveness. Stonewalling. Psychologists John and Julie Gottman describe these communication styles as the "Four Horsemen." When the four are used consistently over time, they have profoundly devastating effects on relationships, and teams rely on relationships.

Being able to identify which horse you ride in on when under stress or in conflict is essential to being able to develop healthier ways of navigating difficult conversations and managing the conflicts that will inevitably emerge on your teams.

Criticism, in this context, is anything but constructive; it is personal and attacks the other person's character. It might sound something like, *"You're careless. You never submit the expense report accurately or on time."*

Frequent criticism paves the way for the second more devastating horseman: Contempt. In her blog post *The Four Horsemen: Criticism, Contempt, Defensiveness, and Stonewalling, Ellie Lisitsa explains,* "When we communicate in this state, we are truly mean—we treat others with disrespect, mock them with sarcasm, ridicule, call them names, and mimic or use body language such as eye-rolling or scoffing. The target of contempt is made to feel despised and worthless. Contempt goes far beyond criticism. While criticism attacks your partner's [teammate's] character, contempt assumes a position of moral supriority over them."[13]

---

[13] Ellie Lisitsa, *"The Four Horsemen: Criticism, Contempt, Defensiveness, and Stonewalling,"* https://www.gottman.com/blog/the-four-horsemen-recognizing-criticism-contempt-defensiveness-and-stonewalling

It may sound something like this: "You never submit the expense report on time or accurately because, clearly, that would just be beneath someone as important as you."

The third horseman and one that is very common is Defensiveness. This is often an automatic reaction to criticism, and it's a response that virtually all of us have engaged in along the way. Others typically experience it as our failing to take responsibility for our actions. We may deflect. We might blame others. We may claim that it was the circumstances, rather than owning our actions. For example, "I couldn't file the expense report because you didn't send me the form." The healthier response is taking ownership of the behavior. "I knew it was due today. I forgot to put it on my calendar. I will take care of it by the end of the day."

Stonewalling rounds out the four horsemen. This occurs when a team member shuts down, disengages, or withdraws. Oftentimes, the team member will stonewall because they do not know how to manage the disagreement or conflict constructively. If you see yourself stonewalling in response to strong emotions or conflict on the team, it can be helpful to take a break and come back to the issue or situation. Stonewalling can become a pattern and a path of least resistance, which can leave important issues unaddressed.

If the team discovers that many of them tend to stonewall, it is essential that they discuss how they will create a structure for addressing the challenging conversations that must be had (see Chapter 4).

Several teams that I've worked with spell out in their team pact, specifically how they are likely to come across to their teammates when they are angry or under stress. They also articulate how their teammates can help them when they are in this emotionally hijacked state. They take ownership for their behavior, as well as express what they are intentionally working on to develop more effective behaviors when they are stressed or angry. It might look something like this example from a team pact:

"When the stress kicks in and the Four Horsemen (Criticism, Stonewalling, Contempt, Defensiveness) *show up bringing dysfunction and toxicity with them, team members shared what their teammates likely will see, what each needs from the others to move out of dysfunction, and what individual team members commit to working toward to effectively mitigate their dysfunctional behaviors:*

What you will see	What I need from the team	What I'm working toward
Alan—Contempt. I get pessimistic, negative, and mean, I'm probably overwhelmed.	I need space—to take a walk, be alone.	I'm calm, strategic, and addressing the overwhelm one bite at a time.
Laurel—Stonewalling. I get very quiet and defensive.	I'm probably overwhelmed. I need the team to ask what they can do to help.	I'm calm and open to change.
Kraig—Stonewalling. I get nervous and very quiet.	I need the team to ask what I need.	I'm seeking input from team members and taking action on what I know I need to do.
Paul—Contempt. I start making quick decisions without input and become condescending.	Call me out.	I am calm and present with the situation that needs to be addressed.
Will—Defensive. I get defensive and start blaming others and pointing fingers.	Be straight with me.	I am focused on problem-solving and taking ownership.

Amber—Defensive. I get defensive and take a command-and-control approach.	Urge me to look at different perspectives, to be less rigid.	I am a calm facilitator. I am present.
Jacob—Contempt and Criticism. I use biting sarcasm, and I will become dismissive of others.	Call it out and urge me to slow down.	I am patient, open, and empathetic.

Step 4 Co-Creation—Defining the Team's Needs, Desires, and Wants

Once the group has had a chance to discuss the team culture they don't want and own the ways in which they may contribute to dysfunction and team toxicity, they are ready to shift gears and talk about the team environment and culture they do want—the one they will commit to co-creating. This is one of the most effective exercises I've used in helping teams clearly articulate what they need from one another and the team as a whole to be successful.

- Follow the steps listed previously.
- Each person should have a stack of Post-it Notes and a black marker.
- Pose this question to the group: **What is the team culture that you will create on this project?**
- This is another rapid-fire exercise, so give them about sixty to ninety seconds to individually come up with as many answers as possible.
- Encourage them to write one idea per Post-it, and keep each to just a couple of words.
- Now it's time for discussion.

You will get numerous answers to the question. For example:

> "Positive." "Reliable." "Trustworthy." "Respectful." "Accountable." "Willing to ask questions." "Do what you say you will do." "Supportive." "Bring your best." "Fun." "Confident."

Additionally, it's likely that a few common themes will emerge. In working with numerous teams over the years, I've found that virtually every team wants four core behaviors: Trust, Communication, Respect, and Accountability. Individual team members may use different terms when describing them, but fundamentally those tend to be the Big Four.

The challenge, however, is that, like dysfunctional behaviors, team members often have very different interpretations of what those effective team behaviors look like in action. Their perspectives and interpretations are heavily influenced by their past experiences, the context of the work, the project or work the team is responsible for, and the culture of the organization. What's important is that the team is defining what the effective behaviors will look like in action on *this* team.

Discuss what key terms mean to individuals and the group. For example, encouraging discussion around how each team member defines the term "respect" generates essential conversations around what is important for each person to feel respected.

On one team that I worked with, the term meant appreciating that everyone has different skill sets and openness to different perspectives and opinions around problem-solving and not jumping to conclusions. For another team, it meant listening, collaborating, correcting in private, and showing empathy.

Respect and disrespect are underlying elements in conversations about trust, communication, and accountability, and respect is an essential thread in weaving the fabric of a high-performance team environment.

An article from *MIT Sloan Management Review* revealed that disrespect is a key contributor to dysfunctional and toxic cultures. "Feeling disrespected at work has the largest negative impact on an employee's overall rating of their corporate culture of any single topic. [W]e found that respect —or the lack thereof —was the single strongest predictor of how employees as a whole rated the corporate culture. [R]espect toward employees rises to the top of the list of cultural elements that matter most." [14]

Creating a team culture of respect, trust, accountability, and communication begins with a conversation of what those behaviors look like to members of the team, and defining that in the team pact.

The following section shows how the culture creation exercise might be articulated in the team pact as Core Team Agreements:

Our Core Team Agreements:
We Engage in Clear Communication:

- Expectations are established—who's responsible for what by when.
- We anticipate problems and we address them. We don't wait for them to become major issues.
- We identify what we need from one another, and we express that.
- We share bad news and good news. We don't avoid the bad news.
- We ask for help.
- "I don't know" is okay and encouraged. But I will find out, get the answer, and learn.

We Build Trust

- We are reliable. We are on time. We do what we say we will do.
- We have one another's backs.

---

[14] Donald Sull, Charles Sull, William Cipolli, and Caio Brighenti, "Why Every Leader Needs to Worry About Toxic Culture," MIT Sloan Management Review, March 16, 2022

- We can go to anyone on the team with questions or requests for help without fear of judgment.
- We trust one another to make good decisions.
- We trust ourselves to make decisions that are within our areas of expertise, and seek input from the others when they are not.
- We trust that when we are away for personal reasons (family, vacation, etc.), the deliverables will get done.
- We do not engage in criticism of other teams—as that does not solve the problem or build psychological safety or trust.

We Are Transparent

- We are honest and approachable.
- We share all information and provide access to information.
- We share what is happening across the project with one another, so that all teammates can learn from one another.

We Are Accountable

- We do what we say we will do/what we are supposed to do.
- We own our mistakes.
- We are disciplined.

We Lead

- We are all leaders.
- We do what needs to be done, whether it's "our job" or not.
- We lead by example.

We Have Fun

- We joke.
- We laugh.
- We have beers together.

- We bring a fun and positive mindset to work. (We bring the weather.)

We Create a Safe Environment—Physically Safe and Psychologically Safe

- It is safe to speak up and raise concerns.
- Safe to ask questions.
- Safe to debate issues.

The Primal Problem

How will you and your team "be" when challenges arise, when stress is testing you at every turn, when unforeseen circumstances arise as they always do? Without clearly articulated agreements in your pact, each team member is virtually guaranteed to revert to their primal mode of protection, i.e. take cover, take control, guard their agenda, shelter their ego. In other words, they will do whatever they deem necessary to cover their backside.

In most cases, it's not that they are "bad" or "selfish" team members. It's merely that they are human beings. After all, the natural state of the brain is to be scanning for danger five times per second. When dysfunction sets in, team members sense danger and will likely look to take cover, and fast. The team pact is the framework that the team can turn to when stress triggers dysfunction and dysfunction threatens to slip into toxicity.

Step 5 There Is No "I" in Team—But There Is "ME"

Now that you have your team purpose, you've discussed what you don't want and spelled out the culture and environment that you are committed to creating, the next step is for each person to share something specific that they believe the team as a whole needs from each individual in order to excel.

The question below is posed to the group, and each person is asked to write down their individual answer and be prepared to share it with the others.

What does the team need from team members to excel on this project?

This question prompts the team members to respond with a big-picture view of what will be beneficial to the group as a whole. The following is an example of what could emerge from the team's responses. This too should be included in the team pact.

To excel on this project, the team needs:

Everyone to make the effort to collaborate, participate in discussions, and speak up. If something is unclear, ask questions. Don't work in silos, even though everyone has their jobs and their areas of expertise. Keep one another in the loop and call one another out on behaviors that are inconsistent with the culture we are creating. Be present, not perfect.

Next, the focus turns to the individual team members to specifically articulate what will be most helpful to them in the months ahead, so that they can best fulfill their commitments to the team as a whole.

What do you need personally from your teammates to excel on this project?

Jacob: I need patience, collaboration, reliability, open-mindedness, hard work, and a willingness to have difficult conversations.

Amber: I need your support, your effort, and your dedication to the project. I need different perspectives from my teammates. I need patience and understanding—I'm still learning as well. I need feedback—sometimes I become rigid in how I want to do things. Call me out.

Paul: I need to get to know my teammates better. I need feedback on how I'm doing and how I can get better, and I need good communication daily.

Laurel: I need support from my teammates and clear communication— what do you expect, what do you need, and when do you need it.

Will: I need communication from my teammates—just be straightforward with me, and no "sandwiching" feedback (first the nice compliment, then the negative comment). If something isn't working, tell me.

Kraig: I need communication, hard work, and to be kept in the loop about what is going on when I miss meetings. (Kraig is assigned to another large project as well.)

Alan: I need feedback/constructive criticism, and respect.

Orthodontics and Teams

For any parent who has invested thousands of dollars in braces for your children, you want the orthodontist to ensure that the beautiful smile now gracing your child's adorable face will remain just as lovely for decades to come.

What we know about teeth and teams is that without intentional effort— a permanent retainer for that beautiful smile or an ongoing commitment for that brilliant team pact— things have a way of returning to the way they were. If you engage in the creation of the team pact and you leave it in your electronic files, the agreements and the momentum that you've generated in the creation process will be lost.

Once a month, put the pact on your team agenda for discussion. Ask the team members to share one area in which they believe the team is crushing it and living the agreement as they said they would. Next, ask the team members to identify another area in which they believe the team is experiencing challenges to the agreement. Ask each person to suggest one or two action steps that the team members could take to better fulfill this portion of the agreement. It is essential that this conversation takes place without judgment, but rather from the standpoint of continuous learning and growth.

Author's Note: If possible, engage a certified team coach to facilitate the team alignment process, as they are trained and equipped to create the environment in which all voices are heard and differing perspectives encouraged. A trained facilitator is another option. What's important in creating the pact is that the environment allows for candid discussion.

CHAPTER 7

STOP FIGHTING FIRES—
START LIGHTING THEM

Delegate. Engage. Coach.

"It always seems impossible until it's done."

—Nelson Mandela

Simone's jaw tightened. Her unblinking dark eyes bore into Jamie's. She was furious. Jamie hadn't followed her very specific instructions. Jamie had tried to explain her reasoning and her approach in handling the client, but Simone cut her off, her words terse, measured, and razor sharp. Simone had spoken to the client the evening before and realized halfway through the conversation that Jamie had not followed Simone's precise protocol for handling the project. Once again, Jamie tried to explain that the situation with this client required a different tactic. Attempting to make her case with Simone was a fatal error in judgment.

The room grew cold, no one breathed, and everyone knew what was going to happen next. Jamie was about to be publicly shamed, dressed down, and made an example of for the rest of the team. Simone expected perfection—her version of it, anyway. Jamie hadn't delivered.

Simone had a reputation for demanding that everyone on her team do things exactly the way she did them. She was the leader, after all, and she knew the "right way" to do the job. She kept everyone on a short leash to ensure "consistent quality." The only thing consistent was the revolving door of employee turnover.

Simone talked about empowering her team, the importance of delegation, and sharing credit. Sadly, she did none of those things. She could talk the talk and knew all the buzzwords. Externally, she was seen as a forward-thinking, dynamic leader, who seemingly everyone wanted to work for. Internally, few employees lasted more than twelve months if they worked for her directly.

Simone was extremely bright, hardworking, and had built her department from the ground up. She cared deeply about the work. Her command-and-control approach had served her just fine in the early days, when the company was much smaller. She consistently produced results, so senior leadership looked the other way when it came to some of her other less helpful behaviors.

But as the organization and her department grew, her focus needed to shift to broader, more strategic goals. Simone needed to get out of the weeds of the day-to-day details. She needed to be lighting fires, not continually fighting them or burning bridges with her team, for that matter. Yet, she held tightly to tasks and responsibilities that, frankly, her employees could execute more effectively. She was working nights, weekends, and taking her computer with her on vacation. She could not bring herself to relinquish control. Her insecurities grew and her leadership approach morphed from a merely difficult command-and-control style to a far more destructive "command-and-crush" approach. Eventually, Simone was removed from the organization, but not before there had been significant collateral damage.

Working Harder Is Hardly Working

As we've learned, the new leader is often placed into a leadership role because they were very good in the position they had, which earned them the promotion. Naturally, they feel tremendous pressure to get this leadership thing right. What they did in their previous job really well is a security blanket, something they knew, and they were known for. But now they have to lead—whatever their interpretation of that may be.

So, many new leaders will leap into hyper-action mode, running and racing here and there day after day, trying to make sure everything gets done just so—the way they do it. They are working harder and harder trying to prove that they are worthy of this "elevated" status, yet getting less and less done.

Moreover, if you talk to their team members frequently, you'll learn that the new leader has a strong desire to be involved in seemingly everything and direct nearly everything. The leader would like to allow the team members to do more, but handing over responsibility for certain tasks is the ultimate struggle, the impossible dream, because so often the leader is trapped in the *"No one does it better than me"* mindset, or the fear of *"If I don't do it, I'll lose control."*

Delegation—Great Idea! Rarely Implemented (Well)

The struggle for new leaders to delegate creates an interesting conundrum. It is critical to effective leadership, yet the thought alone can spark pure dread. It is one of the most anxiety-producing, insecurity-fueling, and necessary actions new (and experienced) leaders must take.

The excuses to avoid doing so are many. Here are a few long-standing favorites: Time—I'm too busy. Perfection—They won't do it right (translation—the way I do it). Guilt—I shouldn't dump more on their plate. Hero—I'm the manager, I should protect them from this hard thing. Victim—If they'd step up, I wouldn't have to do everything. Fear—If I train them to do my work, I won't be needed. It is likely fear that is driving the other excuses as well.

Does any of this sound familiar? If so, you are in good company. The difficulty or failure to delegate is a common trap. But if you're always the one giving orders, answers, instructions, or, worse, swooping in and taking over, you're not setting yourself or your team up for success. Rather, you're sowing the seeds of learned helplessness.

Psychologists Martin Seligman and Steven Maier coined the term "learned helplessness" decades ago.[15] It shows up on teams when employees feel they have little autonomy, authority, or say in how tasks and responsibilities are executed. It also emerges when the leader is the "go-to" person, always directing next steps and telling team members what to do.

Erica discovered this when she went on vacation for a week. She was a recently promoted new leader working in a publishing company. "I just assumed they knew where to focus their priorities. We have some big projects that must get done on a short deadline. But when I returned, several of the team members were working on lower-priority tasks."

Erica's direct reports routinely went to her for instructions on which assignments to pursue next. So, when she wasn't there, they were uncertain how to proceed. It was a perfect example of learned helplessness, in which team members were rendered inert in the leader's absence. Although completely unintended, Erica had created a culture in her department in which no one would make a decision or take initiative without her direct instruction. So they "busied" themselves in her absence with "safe" tasks that were also low-priority activities. It was an important and eye-opening lesson for Erica.

---

[15] "Learned Helplessness: A Theory for the Age of Personal Control," published by Martin Seligman, Lyn Y. Abramson, and John D. Teasdale in 1978.

Serving as department traffic director, keeper of the knowledge, and assigner of projects was now holding both Erica and her team back. In her new role as a leader in the department, she was being asked to take on more complex, strategically focused responsibilities. She couldn't do that if she was continually involved in all the decision-making and directing specifics on projects. She had to equip her team to step up.

In other, more destructive cases, such as with Simone's team, the staff disengaged, checked out, or didn't make much effort because they had little to no authority to take ownership. Not to mention, it was downright risky. If they did try to problem-solve or engage in critical thinking, and Simone didn't have a say or it was a different approach than she would have taken—even if the result was still effective—the employee, as we read earlier, would incur her inexorable wrath.

The Alternative: "DelEngage"

For you to succeed as a leader and your team to excel, you simply must accept that you are not there to do it all, nor are you there to be the ultimate font of knowledge whose wise words and sage advice are the only answers to work's vexing questions, or that your approach is the singular path to successful completion of assigned duties and projects.

In fact, to tell yourself that you must be all that and more is disrespectful to the smart, talented people who surround you. The reality is that it's NOT possible. So stop. Enough. Cease and desist. Rather, recognize that when you delegate, you foster team engagement, hence the term DelEngage. And at the root of DelEngage is, indeed, delegate.

When it is handled with clarity and intentionality, engagement-driven delegation strengthens your and your team's effectiveness because it is about equipping the players on your team for success, identifying the desired outcomes, and creating systems of connection that foster the accountability necessary for you, dear leader, to realize those desired outcomes and strategic goals.

Delegating duties and tasks doesn't mean abdicating responsibility. Rather, it's a means of effectively maximizing all that you and your team have to offer, and it begins with a series of straightforward steps.

Step 1—Identify which tasks and responsibilities to hand off and which ones to keep. Before you panic, I'm not suggesting that you just randomly start rolling responsibilities off your plate and onto someone else's, like those gritty peas that, as a child, you tried to surreptitiously slip onto your sibling's plate without your parent noticing.

Rather, you're taking a strategic, well-considered approach by conducting a time, task, and responsibility inventory. On your phone, computer, or notepad, for one work week, track <u>everything</u> (or at least almost everything) you do relating to your job, such as scheduling, attending meetings, filling orders, talking to clients, collecting data, mediating between warring factions, completing reports, pursuing strategic goals and objectives, providing feedback, serving as office therapist, tracking data, changing lightbulbs, cleaning the office refrigerator. You get the idea. Roughly track how much time those tasks take, and indicate if you are TRULY the ONLY person who can complete them. While you're at it, make a separate list of those items that you should be doing, but never seem to get to because of lack of time, interest, or resources. Keep it real. You don't have to share this list with the world on social media, but it is important that you're not sugarcoating your own reality.

Step 2—After you've gathered your data, objectively look at what is consuming your time. No judgment. Is your day primarily spent on activities that are laser-focused on your department's, team's, or business' goals? Or are you continually putting out fires that wouldn't ignite if you engaged in a bit more planning, communication, and coordination with your team? Are you pulled into situations and activities that repeatedly interrupt your primary responsibility as a leader? Is your list full of items that only you in your position can do? Or do you have a multitude of duties that other employees could and should do? Lastly, are there items on that list that don't belong on anyone's list because they should be outsourced, or are they the result of lack of technology (hello AI), inefficient space, or ineffective processes or systems?

If you discover that your day is consumed with unproductive tasks and responsibilities that others on your team realistically could and should handle, GREAT! Now you can take action because you, the effective researcher that you are, have collected the data. It's not just an irritating inner whisper berating you for not getting work done, or poking you with unhelpful criticism and kicking up your failure anxieties. You have the facts there in front of you.

Step 3—Now that you've identified which duties you can hand off to someone else, outsource, or eliminate, next consider which tasks are on your list that you never seem to get to because you simply—if we're being honest—don't like or are not good at. Or maybe they require deep, focused work, and you're absorbed in lower priority items that you may enjoy, but are actually a distraction from the more important strategic responsibilities that should be getting your attention.

Assuming that these are not tasks that only you can do—like performance assessments—they can be growth and learning opportunities for others. What you keep avoiding, ignoring and pushing to the bottom of your list because it's an energy drainer for you may well be an engaging energy booster and skill development opportunity for a team member.

Step 4—Next, consider your department's goals and objectives. Think in terms of accomplishing those goals through your team members, rather than trying to do everything yourself. Bring your employees into the tent. In other words, share what you've discovered in your time, task, and responsibility data collection exercise. Discuss with the team how appropriate tasks and responsibilities could be distributed, and seek out their ideas and input. Explore their interests and areas of expertise.

Consider what's on your list that could be stretch assignments for hungry team members who want to expand their skill sets. Communicate your vision for their growth, and how this enables the team as a whole to deliver on department, individual, and/or organizational goals more effectively. The more your employees feel they are a part of the department's/organization's total success, the more vested they become in creating it. Helping them grow their skills creates meaningful learning opportunities for your team and enables you to expand your impact and capacity as a leader.

Step 5—Make an effort to delegate the right duties to the right people on your team. Not everyone is suited to every task. Some people are going to handle certain delegated responsibilities better than others because of their work styles and areas of expertise. For example, delegating highly detailed work to someone who tends to thrive more on the big-picture planning side of things may prove to be a challenge. That said, sometimes those challenges are exactly the development opportunities and stretch assignments that are important to this person's larger professional journey and career aspirations.

This goes for you as well. Be aware of responsibilities that you're putting off or ignoring because you don't like them, don't feel confident, or feel uncomfortable executing them. Coaching for performance is an area in which many new leaders feel particularly unprepared. Acknowledge it. Let your team members know it's an area that you're working to develop and follow through. Seek out a coach yourself to help you develop those skills. Enroll in webinars, listen to podcasts, and watch YouTube videos. Read carefully the section in this chapter on coaching. Just don't ignore it and hope that the responsibility will magically disappear.

Step 6—Communicate your expectations. Another key aspect of handing over responsibility of certain duties is ensuring that the employee knows exactly what you want them to do and how you expect it to be done—at least at the beginning. Perhaps no one has been able to meet your standards because no one really knows what they are.

What do you want the outcome to be when you hand over a specific responsibility? For example, if you are going to delegate preparing the monthly report, make sure you've articulated specifically what you want to see in the report, provide a sample, ensure they know where to gather the necessary data, consider if they need a tutorial on some of the technical aspects, and establish check-ins to answer questions and provide feedback along the way to the person developing the report well before the date you need to deliver it.

An alternative approach would be to give general guidelines as to how you want the responsibility carried out, and be willing to let the staff member develop their own plan for carrying out the task and report back to you with their strategy for executing the assignment. This assumes they have the necessary skills to accomplish the task and need minimal instruction and guidance from you. However, be careful not to hand off an assignment and say, "Here you go! Do you understand what to do?" They may understand through their lens, but not yours, so when they deliver the end product, it's nothing like what you expected or what you would have done. The result: You're likely frustrated and ready to retake control, which serves neither of you.

Instead, make sure you're both on the same page regarding what "good" looks like and what the end result should look like. Ask the team member to explain to you what they are going to do, how they are going to carry out the task, and what the outcome will be. That will tell you if they truly do understand what you expect, and just because they may take a somewhat different approach than you would doesn't mean their method is wrong. After all, there's more than one way to bake a cake.

Determine how you will measure your employees' ability to carry out their delegated duties. Everyone who is expected to perform a task must know exactly what goals or targets they're aiming to hit, and how their performance will be measured.

As they become proficient in executing new tasks and responsibilities, they may discover better and more effective ways of performing them. Fantastic! That's a win!

Step 7—Provide the tools and the authority to help the person succeed. Give them the supplies, the materials, the training, and the budget to get the job done right and to make the decisions that need to be made. Be available and encourage questions, but don't hover. If the employee is going to have a chance at effectively carrying out this responsibility, you have to step out of the way. Remember, you're a safety net, not a straitjacket.

Step 8—Create a process for routine connection. Connection fosters accountability. Check in regularly with the person you've delegated a new responsibility to, or ask them to schedule fifteen minutes on your calendar each week, every few days, once a month—whatever the task requires—to provide an update, bring questions, and seek your *constructive* feedback and *instructive* guidance.

Remember, initially they probably won't perform the task as well as you, and it's possible, if not likely, that they will make mistakes. That's part of the learning process. Checking in with them allows you to stay in the loop. Monitor progress and again make sure that this person has the training, time, and resources to complete the assignment according to your expectations. Otherwise, the employee is less likely to succeed, as is your effort to delegate.

Additionally, use this time to help your team member reflect on what they are learning. A few simple questions enable them to consider how they are growing and what they are discovering. For example, ask, "What are you learning?" "What has been challenging/easy?" "What insights can you apply going forward?" "What would you do differently next time?"

Now Celebrate! You can, indeed, effectively "DelEngage"! You're growing your skills and your team's. You're getting work done through others, and, most importantly, you're expanding your capacity as an effective leader.

2. What milestones will mark your progress for each date on your timeline?

3. To whom will you report your success and/or challenges as you complete each milestone?

4. Who can support you when you lose focus, face challenges, or want to give up?

5. How will you celebrate EACH milestone or win—no matter how seemingly small—along the way?

In some cases, the goal may need to be adjusted based on what is discovered in each section. As much as we crave these types of efforts to be clean and linear, they rarely are. That said, the OWN IT model provides a very helpful, action-oriented map to move toward your and/or your team members' dreams and goals.

Fan the Flame

In summary, put DelEngagement and ongoing coaching into action and watch your team grow and your leadership flourish. Remember, what may be an energy drainer for you may well be an energy generator for your team member. More importantly, it's likely to be an opportunity for them to learn and develop. Set both of you up for success:

- Provide the team member with the necessary resources to effectively deliver on the assignment.
- Ensure that you both have a clear understanding of the desired outcome, i.e., defining what successful completion looks like.
- Serve as a resource for advice, feedback, coaching, and assistance as the team member executes the task or responsibility.

Effective delegation is essential to effective leadership. It enables you to expand your capacity and take on bigger and more interesting opportunities because you have equipped your team to take on greater and more challenging opportunities.

Use coaching to create an environment of continuous learning and growth on your team and in service to your department and organizational goals. And when it comes to becoming the effective leader you are capable of being, set your goal and OWN IT!

CHAPTER 8

CURIOSITY IS QUEEN, KING, AND EVERYTHING IN BETWEEN

"It's not impermanence per se... that is the cause of our suffering, rather it's our resistance to the fundamental uncertainty of our situation."

—Pema Chödrön,
Living Beautifully with Uncertainty and Change

Dear Reader, I'd like to introduce you to your new three best friends. They travel in a pack, so plan to involve them as a group. Individually, they don't have the same effect. But when you engage with them together, they can be a source of adventure, exploration, and discovery. They bring endless possibilities, for sure. That's the good news.

Now for the not-so-good news. For all their opportunity and potential for innovation, they are, for many, many new leaders, a source of fear, anxiety, and emotional exposure.

Who are they? Your three best friends as a new leader are the words, "I don't know." I suspect there was a churning in your stomach as you read them, perhaps an audible gasp. Now say them out loud, even if it's through gritted teeth. Now write them down. I'm serious, write down the words "I don't know." It's time to get used to the fact that you really don't know... and that's okay.

Sure, there are lots of things you do know. The sun will rise in the east and set in the west. Broccoli will taste just as bad tomorrow as it does today. Exercise still requires effort. The cashmere sweater will eventually pill. But the list of what you don't know is essentially endless, and the seemingly cruel irony is that we humans hate uncertainty. It's scary.

Our brains equate uncertainty—not knowing—with danger. When our brains sense danger, the smallest and most survival-obsessed part kicks in. That little almond-shaped amygdala wedged deep inside our cranium is launched into combat mode and screaming that you must take immediate action to fight, flee, or freeze. It's leaping to conclusions and hurtling toward worst-case scenarios, and when you don't do what it tells you to do, it piles on with more terrifying imaginary scenes of death and destruction, more tales of doom, gloom, and woe. The sirens are blaring.

Uncertainty is frightening. We don't like it. We also don't like to be wrong. Being wrong is literally painful. In fact, it physically hurts to be wrong.

Studies using fMRI brain imaging have shown that a region involved in processing physical pain is also activated when we experience social or emotional pain, such as embarrassment or shame from discovering we are wrong.[17]

Failing Out Loud

When we must acknowledge that we are wrong or that we don't know the answer, it challenges our belief that *"As the leader with X title*—be it manager, director, team lead, supervisor, take your pick—*I should know."* We set ourselves up for discomfort and, possibly, failure by setting an

---

[17] Naomi I. Eisenberger *et al.*, Does Rejection Hurt? An fMRI Study of Social Exclusion. *Science***302**,290-292(2003).DOI:10.1126/science.1089134

internal expectation that we should have the answers, or that our way is the right way, or that we should be able to anticipate the outcome, or that our interpretation of the data is the correct one.

Then something goes awry, and we are wrong. Our assumptions were wrong. Our numbers were incomplete. Our way of doing things was inefficient or inaccurate. This new information challenges who we thought we were—the leader who was "supposed to know."

Compounding the challenge is the fact that our cultural mythology of leadership has long told us that "leaders" must have the answers. They are the all-knowing, all-seeing decision-makers we look to for the solutions to the vexing problems of life and work. Yet it is that very limited mindset that effectively shrinks the bounty of insight and information readily available to new leaders in the collective intelligence of the groups of colleagues, coworkers, fellow leaders, and others that surround them.

Admittedly, when new leaders "fail" it's usually "out loud." In other words, it's likely to be seen and experienced by at least a few people, maybe several, and some will probably be key stakeholders. Failing certainly isn't fun and, as we know from our own lived experiences and the research, it can be quite painful. However, depending on your attitude, it can also be profoundly instructive.

In her book *Mindset: The New Psychology of Success*, Carol Dweck coined the terms "fixed mindset" and "growth mindset." The growth mindset is a belief that you can get smarter, get better, become more effective with extra effort and investment of time. The fixed mindset is a belief that your basic qualities, like intelligence and abilities, are static, limited, fixed, and cannot be changed.

Those with a fixed mindset:

- Focus on proving themselves.

- Define success as winning.
- Avoid challenges they cannot win.
- Get discouraged easily and give up in the face of obstacles.
- Ignore or dismiss feedback from others.
- Blame others.
- Feel threatened by the success of others.

The mindset may be fixed, but it certainly isn't contained. It bleeds into the surrounding environment. New leaders foster a fixed mindset culture when they fear failure, when they swoop in and take control, rather than letting an employee learn and experiment, when they insist on perfection in themselves and those around them, when they routinely look for what is wrong, rather than what is right. They bridle innovation, creativity, and critical thinking. Team members, if they stay, learn not to experiment, not to push boundaries, not to speak up. They learn to stay small and try to remain inconspicuous to stay safe.

Worse yet, they disengage. According to Gallup, by the end of 2024, employee engagement—the involvement and enthusiasm employees feel toward their workplace—had reached a ten-year low.[18] Nearly 70 percent are "not engaged" at work—meaning they do the minimum required and emotionally detach from their job. They've mentally checked out. Those who are not engaged lack motivation. They don't go beyond basic responsibilities. This disengagement can lead to significant costs for businesses due to decreased productivity, lower morale, and reduced innovation. Gallup estimates that the cost of disengaged employees is a whopping $8.8 trillion in global GDP annually.[19]

---

[18] Jim Harter, "U.S. Employee Engagement Sinks to 10-Year Low," Gallup Workplace, Jan. 14, 2025, https://www.gallup.com/workplace/654911/employee-engagement-sinks-year-low.aspx

[19] Kara Dennison, "Gallup Says $8.8 Trillion Is The True Cost Of Low Employee Engagement," Forbes, July 16, 2024, https://www.forbes.com/sites/karadennison/2024/07/16/gallup-says-88-trillion-is-the-true-cost-of-low-employee-engagement/

Accept No Prisoners

In my work as a leadership development coach, I joke (sort of) that I don't work with "prisoners." The prisoners that I'm referring to, however, are not incarcerated. Rather they are prisoners of their mindset. They are convinced that they have all the answers. They scoff at learning, "What do *I* need to learn? Why, that's for amateurs."

Their way—however ineffective it may be—is the right way. Whatever struggles and challenges they are experiencing are everyone else's fault. They are not willing to look in the mirror and acknowledge that they could grow, develop, and, yes, learn to be more effective.

They are utterly convinced they are right today, tomorrow, to infinity and beyond. They are addicted to the belief that they're right. After all, they've "done it all." They've "tried it all." They've "seen it all," and as a result, they are convinced they know it all.

It's tragic on many levels, as these individuals often have essential skills, experience, and strengths that, if leveraged, could have a significant positive impact on their organizations, teams, and themselves. But they insist that feedback, comments, or complaints about their unhelpful and often destructive behaviors are drivel. "Those people are just too (fill in the blank) ignorant, uninformed, unqualified," they say dismissively. They are convinced—or so they appear—that their frequently antagonistic behavior is effective, has worked for them, is necessary, and should not be questioned. They are not interested in hearing feedback or shining a light on the rocks that they keep tripping over again and again. They are trapped in a fixed and ultimately destructive mindset.

As a result, they don't accept failure or mistakes and often blame others when they occur. They don't venture into unfamiliar territory, refuse to learn new skills, and scoff at recommendations that they change their attitude, let alone their behavior.

Invulnerable, Invincible, and Entitled

Kevin eventually lost his job, but it was well after the organization had invested tens of thousands of dollars in training him, promoting him, praising him, and showering him with lavish bonuses in hopes that he would morph into the leader they so hoped and wanted him to become. He didn't.

Although Kevin wasn't a CEO, or anywhere close to that hierarchical neighborhood, he suffered his own form of "CEO disease." Should a member of his team question him or suggest an alternate approach, Kevin would "educate" them into silence. On and on Kevin would talk about how knowledgeable he was, how experienced he was, how accomplished he was. Eventually, no one on his team would speak up or question him, lest they be subjected to a thirty-minute diatribe on the many ways in which their perspectives, opinions, ideas, and experiences were wrong.

In client meetings, he insisted on being the center of attention, steering the discussion into convoluted, and often inappropriate, areas. He was the court jester, and everyone in the room would be at the mercy of his divergent train of thought, obscure parallels to current events, and general obfuscation when he was confronted with direct questions regarding deliverables and deadlines.

Kevin was a manager who refused to manage. He ignored emails, messages, and phone calls from his team seeking essential information. He showed up late to client meetings. Employees pleaded to be assigned to other areas, some simply quit. When he would receive critical feedback from clients, coworkers, and his boss, he asserted that they weren't "qualified" to evaluate him.

He lamented that he was an "unappreciated perfectionist" who could get a much better and higher paying job somewhere else, he just hadn't decided where. Kevin had no interest in learning how to become a more effective teammate, manager, or leader. He already held an advanced degree, he asserted. Additional learning or so-called continuous improvement, he sneered, was beneath him. It wasn't until he disregarded critical processes that cost the company hundreds of thousands of dollars that he was finally let go.

As Dweck explores in her book, the fixed mindset emerges across multiple spectrums, from school children to professional athletes to intelligent professionals and seemingly brilliant CEOs. In the section *Invulnerable, Invincible, and Entitled*, she describes leaders with a fixed mindset, "They didn't set out to do harm. But at critical decision points, they opted for what would make them feel good and look good over what would serve the longer-term corporate goals."[20]

Kevin's fixed mindset cost him his job. It also cost the organization excellent, highly qualified employees, and at least a few clients.

Growth Is a Choice

Successful leaders look back on their "failures" as powerful learning experiences that forced them to move forward in ways they would have never considered. For these are pivotal periods in which they were soaking in the dark belly of the beast, and they had to come to terms with limitations, shortcomings, and fears.

As the ego berates them for not knowing, not doing, not anticipating, and admonishes them for trying, those with a fixed mindset will retreat to the dim corners of safety and what they've always known. Reinforcing the armor of their self-image, they will pledge to never risk such loss and pain again.

Those with a growth mindset will pick up their learnings, bandage their bruised egos, and humbly make their way back into the light of day. After

---

[20] Mindset The New Psychology of Success, Carol S. Dweck, Ph.D., Ballentine Books, 2016, 122

all, this seemingly horrible thing that happened—feeling foolish, being wrong, making a bad call—actually just opened up a whole new set of experiences and learning opportunities that are ripe for the taking.

When new leaders embrace a "growth mindset" they can acknowledge that challenges are normal and can be overcome. Those with a growth mindset:

- Focus on improving themselves.
- Define success as learning and growing.
- Embrace challenges as opportunities to learn and grow.
- Persevere through obstacles and learn from mistakes.
- Look beyond "either/or" thinking.

Spare the Pity and Welcome Paradox to the Party

In their research on the *microfoundations of organizational paradox*, the authors explore the challenges that leaders and team members face in navigating a seemingly constant state of contradictory demands and the impact of the "paradox mindset." Is it an either/or problem or a both/and opportunity? That depends on your mindset.

The paradox mindset enables you to hold more than one perspective, to explore multiple options. It isn't about just "this or that," but about what is possible when you move beyond an either/or, win/lose, past/future, collaboration/competition, stability/change, learning/performing mindset and hold multiple perspectives and ideas. These "tensions" enable you and your team to explore multifaceted solutions and embrace complexity and creativity.

As a leader you will find yourself in a state of seemingly constant tension as one challenge after another comes at you like pelting rain in a storm. That, my friend, is the very nature of leadership. Trying to eliminate the tensions exhausts your resources. "However, when these tensions are accepted and valued, individuals can gain energy from them and increase their overall available resources for performing their specified jobs."[21]

In other words, those with a high paradox mindset see challenges as opportunities. But they don't stop there, they walk the leadership ledge and invite challenges, specifically from their teams.

The Challenge Mindset

Early in 2021, the global financial services company Credit Suisse and former pillar of Switzerland's financial establishment incurred $5.5 billion in losses following the default of Archegos Capital Management. The catastrophic financial hammering was, in part, the result of "a cultural unwillingness to engage in challenging discussions."[22]

For new and experienced leaders, it takes courageous vulnerability to invite challenges to your thinking, your plan, your ideas, and your strategies. Afterall, you've got that fancy title, and you really want to have the answers.

What's more, we humans, by our very nature, have excessive confidence in our own perspectives, ideas, and opinions. "Myside" bias is our belief that our "way" is superior. Consequently, we're interested in hearing from those who agree with us, not those who challenge our beliefs, opinions, or perspectives—even if they are on the front lines doing the work and would bring valuable insights.

And given our natural tendency to search for information that confirms our opinions and beliefs, it's easy to practice pseudo inquiry. We want to appear open-minded and willing to consider other perspectives, yet, as leaders, we often fail in our execution. We toss out halfhearted, weak little

[21] Kanfer and Ackerman, Microfoundations of Organizational Paradox: Paradox Mindset, Limited Resources and Tensions, Article in Academy of Management Proceedings · August 2017, DOI: 10.5465/AMBPP .2017.10930abstract
[22] "Credit Suisse Group Special Committee of the Board of Directors Report on Archegos Capital Management," PDF file (Zurich: Credit Suisse, July 21, 2021), www.credit-suisse.com.

questions, such as, "Does anyone have anything to add?" "Does anyone disagree?" These feeble attempts to encourage so-called discussion do little to convince team members that a candid challenge to the leader's thinking is both welcome and appreciated. Thus a "keep quiet" culture permeates many teams, with potentially perilous results.

In fairness, leaders may genuinely want to engage their team members' challenges and contradictory perspectives, but struggle to take necessary steps to create an environment in which they successfully do so.

In August 2024, the Imperial College Business School Centre for Responsible Leadership published the white paper, *"Facilitating Constructive Challenge: Concrete ways leaders recruit (and repress) speaking up."* The authors conducted what they describe as a rigorous field experiment in the financial services industry in which they examined the interactions between leaders and their teams.

The study was designed so that the leader would propose a "bad" idea and the team would be observed in real time to see how they reacted to their leader's "bad" idea. Would the employees openly disagree with the leader and challenge their thinking or agree with them and send the idea on as proposed?

The authors analyzed more than thirty hours of transcript data identifying the strategies that leaders used and how their teams responded. They compiled a series of steps leaders can take to invite challenges and deepen discussions on their teams.

First, what didn't work. General questions, such as "What do you guys think?" "Anybody else want to contribute?" These questions generate about a 50 percent likelihood that someone is going to challenge the leader. Asking a specific person who is accountable for the outcome to weigh in yields a slightly lower response. Pleading requests for input, such as, "Any ideas? Any other thoughts? Anyone?" are equally ineffective. Asking about implementation and next steps still didn't encourage challenges to the leader's intentionally "bad" idea. In fact, the likelihood of someone speaking up in disagreement dropped to 44 percent.

So what can leaders say that will not only invite, but encourage much-needed challenging dialogue on plans, ideas, strategies and the like?

The authors found that asking specifically for disagreement gives team members permission to challenge their leader's opinions, ideas, plans, strategy, perspectives, etc. If the boss is asking to be challenged, the team members are giving the leader what they are asking for. Conversely, when team members are asked if they agree with the leader, they feel more pressure to do so. Let's face it, to challenge or disagree with the boss feels like a risk. Most of us learn early on that pleasing the boss, doing what they ask, following the BBSS rule (because the boss said so), is the way to ensure the bills are paid.

"The most effective strategy asks for challenge specifically, without putting the spotlight on the individual. When leaders asked their teams questions that requested input about what could prevent an idea from being executed successfully, this increased the likelihood that one of their team [members] would challenge to 59 percent."[23] Although it is the most effective, the authors found it was rarely used.

Ding, Ding, Ding!

The bells should be ringing in your head. This is your opportunity, new leader, to ensure that you are getting the best out of your team and your leadership. Make it a practice to invite challenges regularly. Make it clear to your team that disagreement, speaking up, expressing dissenting opinions is not only necessary, but also required. Then, dear leader, actually listen and acknowledge the opposing view, the additional information, the different perspective. You don't have to love it, but you do have to

---

[23] C. Moore, K. Coombs, M. Gao, et al., "Facilitating Constructive Challenge: Concrete Ways Leaders Recruit (and Repress) Speaking Up," PDF file (London: Imperial College Business School, August 2024), https://imperialcollegelondon.app.box.com.

welcome it and truly consider it, that is, if you want your team to trust that you really do want and expect them to speak up. In doing so, you can create a culture of respectful dialogue that seeks the best outcome.

What's more, your team is more likely to be engaged contributors because they feel their input matters and their perspectives are respected. As a result, more people will speak up more often, rather than just the one or two who always agree with you anyway.

A word of caution. If inviting challenge and disagreement is new behavior for you as a leader, expect skepticism and resistance. The first few times—maybe even several times—you experiment with this approach, it's quite possible that you will get little interaction. But your persistence will pay off.

Curiosity as a Mindset

"Curiosity will conquer fear more than bravery will."

—James Stephens, Irish poet-storyteller

Jeremy found himself in a leadership position suddenly. He was a mere three months into a new job when his boss left the company for another opportunity. Not only was Jeremy working in a new job, but he was also now working in a new industry. New job, new industry, and now, at thirty-three years old, he was named as the new CFO. Additionally, the organization he was now helping to lead was undertaking significant process changes and experiencing staff turnover.

Jeremy prides himself on being curious, open-minded, and respectful of the expertise of those on his team. "When I came into this role, I knew that I wasn't the expert on any of the things that were changing. So my approach with the team was to say, 'You've been doing this a long time. I'm looking for your ideas on the solution.' I think that was what allowed us to really cement as a team. They were able to say, 'This is my recommendation for this process.' Then we would evaluate it as a team and talk about what could work with their recommendation and what we need to adjust to better serve our customer—the company."

Jeremy's approach required an extraordinary level of vulnerability and courage. "It was tough to admit that I didn't know, and that I didn't have the answers. You expect yourself to know everything, the reality is you can't. I had to put my pride away and focus on what was best for everybody."

It was an approach that, in hindsight, he says, served him very well. "Admitting when I don't know is what has helped me the most. When you pretend to know everything, you don't learn anything. Working with those who are the experts and asking a lot of questions, not only allows you to learn, but it also allows the experts to rethink some of the reasons why things are done a certain way."

Jeremy has created a culture of dialogue and curiosity across his team. "We have weekly team meetings where we talk about what's going on both at work and personally. We check in on what we're working on that week. We bring up issues and challenges that we're running into to the team and talk about them. We also check in on our quarterly and annual goals. It allows us to address barriers that are getting in the way and make adjustments if we need to. We don't save stuff up. We don't push things to the side; we work on things and address issues as they come up, because we can address them a lot more effectively if we're not pushing them to the side."

He credits his curious leader approach to two highly effective leaders whom he had worked for previously. "The CFO I worked for in my last job would come to me and ask my opinion on something or how I would do something. He knew the answer. But he always wanted to hear what I thought and what my recommendations were. That approach helped me to learn and develop very quickly. He wasn't saying 'go do this.' It was 'what do you think we should do here?' He would challenge you to think it through, and if you got stuck, he would always help you."

Jeremy benefited and learned in a culture of curiosity. He's now creating that on his own team.

Invite Curiosity to Foster Collaboration

Getting the work done in today's complex and matrixed organizations often requires leaders to rely on assistance from a diverse collection of employees who don't report to them. They must collaborate to achieve the larger organizational goals. Effectively collaborating means breaking down the proverbial silos. Breaking down the silos, or at least creating an environment where the group can see over them, requires that individuals across multiple departments are aligned to achieve clearly articulated common objectives that are in service to the organization as a whole, not just their individual departments.

To achieve the best outcome, not just any outcome, demands that leaders actively invite challenge and disagreement. In their research, consultants Jonathan Hughes, Jessica Wadd, and Ashley Hetrick emphasize that "Leaders need to walk the talk and provide living examples of how people can change their plans or position on an issue because they embraced disagreement and actively sought out different viewpoints—especially from people lower in the organizational hierarchy and from different business units, functions, and geographies."[24]

Given our addiction to being right and our innate need for certainty, seeking different viewpoints requires intentional practice and a learning mindset.

Try this exercise to strengthen your openness to listening to others' perspectives.

---

[24] Jonathan Hughes, Jessica Wadd, Ashley Hetrick, "Why Influence is a Two-Way Street, Managers achieve better outcomes when they prioritize collaborative decision-making over powers of persuasion," MITSloan Management Review, Nov. 19, 2024, https://sloanreview.mit.edu/article/why-influence-is-a-two-way-street/

First, the next time you're in a conversation, ask yourself the following questions:

- Am I listening to defend, resist, or control?
- Am I listening to problem-solve or correct?
- Am I listening to win?
- Am I not really listening, but simply waiting to talk?

Start to notice how you listen and if you actually do listen.

Second, during at least one conversation a day, commit to use listening to truly connect with the other person. Do this:

- Notice their tone of voice, inflection, body language, facial expressions, energy level.
- Don't interrupt.
- Pay attention to what's not being said.
- Notice the other person's energy—are they calm, concerned, cautious, anxious, tentative, excited, relaxed, happy, etc.?
- Reflect on what you noticed when you truly listened. What did you discover about the issue?
- How did truly listening affect your response?

Third, prepare to invite challenge and discussion.

- Create a list of open-ended questions that begin with either the word "what" or "how." Use the list here to get you started. Bring *a few* key questions from your list to your next conversation, challenge, discussion, or team meeting.
  - What do we need to know about this challenge/issue/ opportunity?
  - What do you think we should do?
  - What's another option?

- ○ How might this fail?
- ○ How might this succeed?
- ○ What assumptions are we making?
- ○ What are four possible options?
- ○ And what else?
- ○ What's most important here?
- ○ How do we make the most of this opportunity/challenge/ situation?
- ○ What would we do if we could?
- ○ What are our top priorities?
- ○ Who's doing what by when?
- ○ When we look back on this in 6, 12, 18 months, what will we wish we had done/considered/evaluated?
- ○ If this initiative fails terribly, what will we wish we had discussed today?
- ○ If this initiative is wildly successful, what will we have done to ensure success?
- ○ What are we missing?
- ○ Whose perspectives, opinions are we not considering?
- ○ What data are we relying on? How might it be wrong?
- ○ What data are we missing?
- ○ How do you feel about this?

Fourth, experiment with the 80/20 rule. Try to genuinely listen 80 percent of the time and talk 20 percent of the time. And finally, seek to be an explorer rather than an expert. Leave your biases, assumptions, and personal opinions at the door. The most effective leaders have or develop insatiable curiosity. They're listening to learn, not merely waiting to talk.

CHAPTER 9

ACE YOUR CONNECTIONS

"The deepest principle in human nature is the craving to be appreciated."

—William James,
father of American psychology

Jillian had spent months working with local community members in an effort to educate key constituent groups on the importance of a small tax increase that was earmarked specifically to upgrade public facilities that were in serious, and frankly dangerous, disrepair. With family members actively using these public facilities, Jillian had a personal connection to the effort. In addition to her full-time day job, she worked tirelessly on the effort, organizing focus groups, building alliances, canvassing neighborhoods, hosting meetings, the list went on and on.

But Jillian had another important reason to invest her time. If the tax increase passed, it would significantly benefit her employer, a company that provided services to the local government. So her boss happily supported her efforts, and Jillian kept him apprised of what she was doing on a regular basis.

When the increase passed by a significant margin, Jillian's boss announced the win to the organization and what it could mean financially for the company. It was significant, and he took full credit, noting his personal relationships with key leaders in the community, never acknowledging Jillian's grassroots efforts. At the time, Jillian took the slight in stride, dismissing it as an unintentional oversight. "It hurt. A small thank you or even a 'good job,' would have been nice. But, oh well," she said.

Over time those unintentional oversights, seemingly insignificant slights, and misunderstandings break down relationships. Connections that are frayed will unravel.

As Annie Dillard says, "How we spend our days, is, of course, how we spend our lives."[25] According to industrial-organizational psychologist Andrew Naber, the average person—that would be you, your team, your boss, your colleagues and coworkers—will spend ninety thousand hours at work over their lifetime.[26] You want to know that your work matters. That your contributions are valued and appreciated. So, too, do your team members. In fact, your team will walk through fire for you if they know you care. They will also walk away—be it physically or emotionally—if they know—or strongly suspect—that you don't.

In the final chapter of this book, I discuss the process of letting go and what prompts some excellent and highly effective leaders, employees, and team members to leave their organizations.

But for now, our focus is on keeping them and you in rewarding and enriching jobs in which appreciation and acknowledgement for good work, hard work, and committed work are simply the way things are done.

Appreciate Profit More Than Loss

Showing appreciation as part of a rewarding employee experience isn't just a charming, warm, fuzzy, feel-good idea. It's the difference between

---

[25] Annie Dillard, *The Writing Life* (Harper & Row, 1989).

[26] Gettysburg College. (2023). *One third of your life is spent at work*. Gettysburg College. https://www.gettysburg.edu/news/stories?id=79db7b34-630c-4f49-ad32-4ab9ea48e72b

profit and loss. Each year, Willis Towers Watson, a global financial services company, surveys more than five hundred companies and nearly ten million employees to better understand what truly drives a high-performance employee experience.

In 2019, the company released its first Willis Towers Watson HPEX (High Performance Employee Experience) white paper. In it, the authors defined four key dimensions that would be considered table stakes or fundamentals that employees are looking for on the job:

- Work—Doing great work in a thriving organization
- Reward—Growth and reward opportunities in return for that great work
- People—Connection with great people and leaders
- Purpose—A strong sense of purpose

From WTW's list of five hundred client companies, only those that achieve strong financial performance and strong employee survey performance make the list of high-performance companies. This is not an easy bar to clear by any stretch, but the return on investment is huge. "Had you invested $1,000 in the market in general [in 2002], it would now [2017] be worth just over $2,000. However, had you invested in our group of high-performance companies, your $1,000 would now be worth nearly $9,000."[27]

Beyond the fundamentals, high-performing companies excel in four key areas:

- Inspiration—Clear vision and strategy, belief in purpose, values driven behavior

---

[27] Stephen Young, Patrick Kulesa, Willis Towers Watson-HPEX Breakthrough Research White Paper, 2019

- Trust—Open and honest communication, confidence in leadership, integrity, and respect
- Drive—Customer driven, change effectiveness, speed and agility in the market
- Recognition—Transparent rewards, pay equity, pay for performance, tailored compensation and benefits

Companies with a more engaging employee experience outperform their peers for top-line growth, bottom-line profitability, and return to shareholders. According to the 2024 update to the Willis Towers Watson Breakthrough Research white paper, "… high-performing organizations achieved nearly three times the revenue growth, 11 times the profit margin, and two times the return on equity compared to global averages." [28]

The numbers are clear. It pays to invest in creating an engaged workforce. Employees crave meaningful connection to their work and the people they work with. And when it is present, that connection is a powerful differentiator for you as a leader, your department, and your organization's bottom line.

As Kevin Kruse describes it in his book *Employee Engagement 2.0*, "Engaged employees work harder and longer with more focus, [which] increases productivity, increases service, increases quality, [creates] more satisfied customers, more sales, more profit, higher stock share price, higher total shareholder value." [29]

You Hold the ACE

ACE your connections and you'll build bonds with your team that can withstand the stress and strain that are the very fabric of our world of

---

[28] It's official: Great employee experiences (still) result in superior financial performance, Jill Havely, Angela Paul, Lindsay Stortz and tiffany Shortridge, Ph.D., Feb. 26, 2024

[29] Kevin Kruse, Employee Engagement 2.0: How to Motivate Your Team for High Performance: A Real-World Guide for Busy Managers (Richboro, PA: The Kruse Group, 2012, 11

work. ACE stands for acknowledge and appreciate often, course correct as needed, set clear expectations and evaluate.

While setting clear expectations and course correction are essential in ensuring that your team members are set up to succeed and have the tools to deliver on the job, acknowledgement and appreciation fuel the engine of high performance. What's more, they help reinforce what the team members are doing right, as well as strengthen an environment of ongoing dialogue. Therefore, when you have to have the difficult and challenging conversations because—well, that's just life and work —the other person is likely to be far more receptive.

Your most effective, dedicated, loyal, and hardworking team members already have intrinsic motivation. They do the work well because they see value in what they do. However, if you rarely speak to them. If they feel like they are on an island. Worse, if you're working in the same building, down the hallway, and the only time you talk to them is if you happen to cross paths in the break room, that intrinsic motivation will only sustain them for so long.

Matt had worked for his employer for more than five years. Early on, he had what he considered to be an excellent relationship with his boss. They checked in regularly. He received consistent constructive feedback and helpful guidance on projects that he was working on. "It was clear that the work I was doing really mattered to the organization, and it was openly valued by my boss."

Then, seemingly overnight, Matt felt like he and his work were no longer relevant or valued. "My boss essentially disappeared. We went from having almost daily conversations to going weeks with little more than a perfunctory 'Hi, how are you?' when we ran into one another in the kitchen. It was really disconcerting. I should have done something sooner and reached out. But I stewed."

Matt says that a new person had joined the leadership team who saw Matt's work as far more transactional than his boss had seen it.

Eventually Matt insisted on regular one-on-one time with his boss. But the tide had shifted. What was once a very positive and supportive relationship had clearly soured. Matt had invested thousands of dollars of his own money and hundreds of weekend hours in continuing his education. He was intrinsically motivated, loved his work, and had been instrumental in shaping an employee-centric culture in the organization. But after two more years of what he describes as little to no appreciation, gaslighting, and a significant shift to a top-down corporate culture, he left the organization for a better opportunity.

Appreciate to Motivate and Innovate

Praise and appreciation from managers consistently score as a top motivator for performance. In fact, 67 percent of workers just want a little gratitude for their hard work. What's more, 69 percent say they would work harder if they felt their efforts were recognized. It costs nothing, and while 78 percent of employees surveyed say that appreciation motivates them in their job, a full 65 percent of Americans report receiving no recognition during the past year at their work.[30]

Managers are often focused on their own work, the "problem children," and the high potentials. The rest—the vast majority who are making sure the work is done, the clients are taken care of, the essential operations of the business are churning—are often overlooked. It's easy to overlook them. They don't require much, and they typically ask for even less. Then they leave, and you're suddenly left without a key contributor and thinking, *Wait, what?*

According to Quantum Workplace's 2024 report on employee engagement, *Not Another Employee Engagement Trends Report*, engaged employees are more likely to say their workplace has a positive culture that impacts their own work, as well as how they behave. Disengaged employees, on

[30] "Top 12 Employee Appreciation Statistics," Baudville, Feb. 21 2022, https://ideas.baudville.com/top-12-employee-appreciation-statistics/

the other hand, are 2.6 times more likely to seek out opportunities where they perceive the culture is better.

What's more, creating a culture of appreciation doesn't require some grand plan. Too often, we're overthinking it and making it more difficult and cumbersome than it needs to be. And that becomes an excuse to ignore, dismiss, and disregard it. Although it might be nice, we don't need a formal recognition program to extend thanks and appreciation to those who make us, our departments, teams, projects, and organizations successful.

Appreciation is a grassroots endeavor. You create and reinforce a culture of appreciation in how you interact with your team, your attitude, what you acknowledge as important, how you communicate, how you listen, and the list goes on.

Simply start by calling attention to what team members are doing well—be that executing a process, handling a client effectively, raising a challenging issue in a team meeting, experimenting with a new procedure, or helping another teammate with a large project. The list of possibilities is virtually endless. These modest acts of acknowledgement alone help to motivate and fuel engagement. Moreover, appreciation greases the wheels of psychological safety, which props open the door to innovation. Team members are more likely to step up and step out of their comfort zones when they feel appreciated.

As Harvard Business School professor and author of *The Fearless Organization* Amy Edmondson defines it, "Psychological safety is a belief that one will not be punished or humiliated for speaking up with ideas, questions, concerns, or mistakes, and that the team is safe for interpersonal risk taking."[31]

---

[31] Amy C. Edmondson, "Psychological Safety and Learning Behavior in Work Teams," *Administrative Science Quarterly* 44, no. 4 (December 1999).

Acknowledge what your team members are doing well, and you build mutual trust and respect. Where there is appreciation, trust, and respect, there is greater confidence. When team members feel confident, they innovate, make valuable contributions, share critical opinions, and new ideas. They are also more likely to acknowledge missteps and seek to continuously improve as team members in service to one another, the goals, and the organization's mission.

What "Language" Are You Speaking?

In their book *The 5 Languages of Appreciation in the Workplace*, authors Gary Chapman and Paul White identify five different ways in which employees typically like to be shown appreciation. You can learn specifics about your and your team's appreciation preferences by taking their Motivating by Appreciation assessment.

Here are a few of the languages that they discuss in their book.

Words of Affirmation

This is about speaking words of acknowledgement and appreciation and verbally affirming a positive characteristic about a person, such as perseverance, commitment, positivity. This might be an achievement or accomplishment, or perhaps the team member executed a process exactly according to specifications.

If you're consistently looking for what your team members are doing right, you'll find many opportunities to verbally acknowledge and appreciate their work. Catch them in the act of doing good and call it out, specifically naming what they did. For example, "Liz, you handled Mrs. Smith's complaint this morning with respect and integrity. Your approach has a significantly positive impact on our brand. Thank you."

This makes it clear to Liz what she did well, when, with whom, and the impact. In other words, it's specific. It's not a broad brushstroke comment like, "Nice work with that customer." While general acknowledgement is better than nothing, it's weak and likely forgotten or worse, dismissed as insincere. To deliver praise in a way that will be far more meaningful takes about thirty seconds of forethought and less than thirty seconds to deliver. It costs nothing, but the impact will make you rich. Most importantly, it enables you as the leader to consistently reaffirm the actions and behaviors that you are looking for in your team.

Now for those of you (cynics) who might be getting all worked up and defensive and rolling your eyes, thinking that now you have to commend Joseph for turning on the lights, I have one word for you. STOP. That's not what I'm saying. The point is that if you are intentional and genuine in extending gratitude and appreciation to your team for good, excellent, and quality work in multiple forms, you're demonstrating that you truly value their contribution. You need them to feel appreciated and valued because they enable you to get the work done and have the impact you are capable of having as a leader.

Quality Time

Quality time has many interpretations. Some employees want a few minutes with their boss. Others want time with their colleagues. But, fundamentally, it's about giving your undivided attention, not looking at your phone, and actually showing genuine interest in the other person. The authors note that it's also one of the most misconstrued forms of showing appreciation. "Speaking the language of Quality Time to your team is a powerful yet largely misunderstood tool for managers. In the past, many supervisors have interpreted employees' desire for quality time as an inappropriate desire to be their friend or an effort to 'get in good' with the boss...this is seldom the attitude of the employee...[they] simply want to feel that what they are doing is significant and that their supervisor values their contribution."[32]

---

[32] Gary Chapman and Paul White, *The 5 Languages of Appreciation in the Workplace: Empowering Organizations by Encouraging People*, Kindle, (Chicago: Northfield Publishing), 101.

Matt, whom I mentioned earlier in the chapter, was routinely dealing with highly confidential, sensitive, and often difficult employee issues. Simply having his boss come in and check on him periodically would have made a significant difference to Matt feeling that his work was valued. "My supervisor only had seven direct reports. I didn't expect him to hold my hand or spend hours with me. I just wanted him to stop in once in a while and ask how I was doing, and maybe give me a few minutes to bounce some ideas off him. My work was pretty intense at times."

Shared experiences offer a multitude of ways to engage in quality time with your team. These can be anything from lunches with coworkers, ball games with staff, leadership retreats, working with colleagues on special projects, listening sessions, volunteer initiatives such as cleaning up a nearby park, small group dialogues, and coffee and questions with the boss, etc.

One of the organizations I worked for during my career arranged for the consulting team, all of whom worked remotely, to meet in a beautiful location to map out the strategy for the coming year. It was energizing to have a voice in developing the plan for the year, and it wasn't all work. There were several activities that allowed the consultants, who flew in from all over the country, to get to know one another, from horseback riding to kayaking to a "shopping competition." These were productive and engaging team retreats that allowed us to participate in small group strategy sessions as well as fun excursions with one another and the CEO.

Another organization made it a point to create two company-wide events a year. The events were one way to connect the entire team and communicate the message of one organization. The first event was the team appreciation party, and it was held in late winter or early spring. The entire team and their partners were invited, including retirees. It was the opportunity to connect with one another, share an excellent meal and entertainment—from hypnotists to "gambling" to a circus. It also provided a forum for the president to present his vision for the organization and acknowledge the team's hard work throughout the year.

The second event was held in midsummer. This event was all about team building, camaraderie, and communicating an important company message. The focus was twofold: First, bring together the entire organization and create cross-departmental teams to engage in some friendly competitive games. This allowed everyone to get to know one another and build relationships across the company. Second, center the friendly competition on a key element of the organizational culture or a key initiative, such as the core values, the strategic plan, the year's marketing theme, and the like.

While events are nice, they can be expensive, and they are not for everyone. But there are numerous ways in which quality time can be used as a powerful and highly effective means of demonstrating appreciation. Most importantly, it doesn't need to require an inordinate amount of your time or budget.

Acts of Service

This essentially is about stepping up and helping a team member who is or may be struggling, has too much on their plate, or could use some assistance.

If you have some extra time, this is a meaningful way to show appreciation to a team member. Just remember, as the authors emphasize, you probably will need to sincerely ask if you can help more than once. Most of us have an automatic response to say no when someone offers to help us. We usually assure them that we've got this! If you offer your help genuinely more than once, the other person will be more likely to accept your generosity. Be sure you actually have time to help and will finish what you start. And be sure to get clarity from the other person as to exactly what they would like you to do and how they want it done. Avoid the desire to swoop in, take over, and show them how you think they should be completing this task.

Take a Breath and Experiment

Dear new leader, if you feel like you're teetering on the ledge with all this appreciation responsibility, you can breathe a sigh of relief. It's not all on you, boss. It's utterly unrealistic to ask, much less expect, leaders at any level—let alone new leaders—to be solely responsible for acknowledging all the great work that is happening around them. For one, they would need a completely omniscient overview of all actions, interactions, and everything else in between, which is plainly impossible.

In reality, colleagues and coworkers play a significant and important role in employees' feeling engaged and appreciated. They are instrumental in creating a culture of belonging in an organization, in a department, or on a project team. Their appreciation is as valuable, and in some cases, more valuable, than receiving appreciation, kudos, and accolades from the boss.

Follow a few simple steps and begin to experiment with your team to shape the culture of appreciation and acknowledgement that will be most meaningful to you and them.

1.   Have a conversation! Ask them! This isn't confidential information. Ask your team members how they would like their good work to be acknowledged. You can include a question as part of your regularly scheduled check-in meetings. Use it as an icebreaker question in your next team meeting. Create a simple survey and give them a list to choose from that includes a few ideas, such as personal notes or emails, lunch with the team, a gift card to their favorite coffee shop, a flexible Friday, pitching in to help with a tiresome task, the possibilities are endless. You may need to establish a few parameters—that fifty-thousand-dollar bonus might be a stretch. And studies show more money isn't much of a motivator, anyway. Give them the option to add their own ideas.

2. Together read *The 5 Languages of Appreciation* and clearly define what appreciation looks like to your team.

3. Make appreciation part of your regular routine—a habit. Build it into your meetings. If necessary, include a daily reminder on your calendar to acknowledge at least one person's good work.

4. Don't assume that the way you like to be appreciated goes for your team members. Similarly, don't assume that your team members all want appreciation in the same way. Just because Sherrie and Linda work closely together, it doesn't mean that they share the same language of appreciation.

Course Correction

"Culture is created by the worst behavior the leader tolerates."

—Steve Gruenert and Todd Whitaker,
School Culture Rewired

Looking the other way when team members are not performing up to standards or are engaging in behaviors that undercut the culture, values, and mission of your organization, team, or department will almost instantly undermine all your efforts around appreciation and foster an environment of mistrust.

Too many leaders avoid providing course correction for their team members until the problem has become seriously damaging. As Cassie discovered in Chapter 4, by then, the chances that the issue will be handled poorly increase exponentially because the pressure to make the behavior stop now becomes overwhelming.

Your team members CANNOT read your mind. Don't let issues go unaddressed. They are much easier and much less messy when they are handled promptly. Revisit Chapter 4 to put Compassionate Candor to work. In the meantime, here are a few additional reminders.

Pause

Be mindful of your approach and that starts with checking in with what is driving you. We don't like to admit it, but sometimes we are propelled by motives that are less than helpful and even toxic. If your underlying reason for the course correction conversation is to prove that you are smart, right, better, more important, and so on, you will be far more likely to deliver the message in a way that backfires—and damages your relationship with the person, their relationship with the team, and their respect for you, the team, and the organization.

1. Leave the judge and jury to the courtroom and keep your harsh verdicts and absolute statements out of the conversation. If you say to someone, "It's clear, you just don't care about the work," you are reaching a verdict about them, and they will feel attacked. The smallest and least sophisticated part of the recipient's brain is going to kick in, and they will become defensive, lash out, or shut down. Your course-correcting message will not be received.

2. Don't pretend to be the world's spokesperson. "Everyone thinks you are not communicating clearly what you need." You do NOT know what everyone is thinking. Your intuition might be pretty darn good, but it's not *that* good. Once again, the person will become defensive and will not effectively receive what you are trying to share with them.

3. You are not a mind reader. Avoid saying things like, "I know that you're upset about Tom's promotion." You might strongly suspect the reason behind their behavior, but unless the person has told you directly why they are reacting or behaving the way they are, you are likely to be bringing your assumptions and best guesses into the room, and there is a very good chance that those guesses are merely your fantasies about why the person is behaving in a certain way.

Most importantly, remember: If your motivation is to help your team member become a more effective and valued contributor and you approach the dialogue from a place of compassionate candor, you will be far more likely to be successful in your course-correction feedback delivery.

Expect and Evaluate

Set clear expectations from the start. I cover this in greater detail in Chapters 3 and 7. Here are a few additional questions to consider as you're establishing expectations and evaluating work performance.

- Is the employee clear on what quality work looks like? Have you told them what your quality expectations are?

- Is the employee meeting deadlines and delivering their work in a timely fashion? Have you told them specifically when you need work done? Telling your team member that you need it "as soon as possible" is subject to interpretation. Telling them that they can get it to you when they have time sends the message that it's not a priority. Even if you don't have a hard deadline, agree with the team member when they should have the project or completed task to you.

- Does the team member demonstrate that they have the skills to complete the job they are in? If not, are they being trained to develop the necessary skills?

- Does the team member act like a team member? In other words, do they demonstrate support for the larger team goals and are not singularly focused on just their job? Do they step up and help their teammates and acknowledge their teammates' contributions? Are they someone that you want on the team?

Making the effort to ACE your connections will have a profound and powerful impact on your success as a new leader and a valued member of the organization.

CHAPTER 10

TIME TO SAY GOODBYE?
VALUES ARE YOUR GUIDE

"When I let go of what I am, I become what I might be."

—John Heider,
The Tao of Leadership

I am a recovering workaholic. The truth is, I like to work—okay, I love to work. It gives me joy, satisfaction, a feeling that I'm having an impact, a sense of accomplishment, as well as at least the impression of control. And when it comes to work, I am all-in. I pour myself into my work like a new mother pours herself into her new baby, spending hours fawning over it, feeding and investing in it, nurturing and studying it. Work becomes every fiber of my being, all of me.

I was raised in a household of six children in which hard work was prized. We were expected to get into the workforce as soon as it was legally allowed. For me, I had just finished eighth grade when I took my first job working "on the line" in a sandwich shop. Education was secondary and average grades were fine.

What was most important was making sure that we were on time and never missed a day of work, no matter what else might be going on in our lives. If we were sick, well, we had better be teetering on the edge of death. Work always came first. We weren't expected to be at any special occasions—family weddings, funerals, Thanksgiving, Christmas—unless we happened to be off work.

Work wasn't something you did. It defined who you were, your character, your morals, your worth as a human, your values. I didn't wrap my head around that last part—values—until years later.

The Switch Flips

At various stages in the earlier days of my career, I could sense when things were, shall I say, "icky," i.e., interactions that left me feeling something in between uncomfortable and distraught. Whether it was lewd comments and inappropriate stares or demands that, even for a workaholic, were utterly unreasonable and unrealistic, like the new CEO declaring that she expected 24/7 availability and "nothing short of perfection from everyone." Then there was the organization in which staff actively labored to sabotage other employees' character and their programs in hopes that they could get a larger share of the budgetary pie.

I would grin and bear it for a while, telling myself I couldn't do anything about it. This was why it was called work, I reasoned. I had a mortgage, car payments, two young kids. I would quietly lecture myself, *Keep your head down. Power on. You can't give up. Grit will get you through.* Then, as if a switch would flip, I would be done. I'd wake up and realize that I had reached a breaking point. My challenging, joy-filled work had morphed into demoralizing projects, toxic interactions, and hollow duties. The meaning of the work was gone, and the sense of accomplishment had evaporated. My soul was being slowly crushed. My values were being stomped upon like a line of Riverdance performers pounding out their thumping routine.

Years later, I would look back on these periods of professional transition and recognize that it wasn't some overnight epiphany that enabled me to finally see the light of what was going on around me. Rather, it was that I was finally willing to stop pretending and face the fact that it was time to move on. Long before my so-called switch flipped, I could see it. I could feel it from miles away, months, if not years in advance. The transition train was coming. The steady drumbeat of its metal wheels on the tracks was pulsing in the distance. But I would cover my ears and look away. I didn't want to acknowledge it because whatever this coming shift was, I knew it was going to require that I make often frightening changes. It didn't care that I was scared. It was coming for me anyway.

It comes for you, as well, with each professional—and personal—transition. But as is so often the case, the fear and anxiety are likely to be far, far greater and more ominous than the reality of the forthcoming transformation of your circumstances.

Off the Ledge

I like to say that seemingly unwelcome change is the Universe's way of moving us in the direction that we are supposed to go in this life and on this leadership journey. We resist. The Universe persists. First, it nudges us with the subtle clues; things aren't adding up. We ignore the signs, make excuses, look the other way. We don't get the message, so the Universe ups her game and pushes us harder. It's more obvious now.

Yet we still resist, gripping tighter to what we think we know, what feels safe, and we tell ourselves that we must be interpreting these situations wrong. All the while, we're making convincing arguments to the person in the mirror, saying we don't have choices; there are no other options. We simply must endure. And then the Universe has had enough of our wallowing in self-pity and helplessness and shoves us off the ledge. We are forced to leap into the unknown, take chances, and decide if we are going to be a victim of circumstances or the creator of our reality.

We really do get to decide, and deciding begins with understanding what you value at your core and what matters most to you at this point on this wild ride that is life and work.

Your values are not fixed. It is likely they will change throughout your life and career as your priorities change. However, it is important that you get clarity on what they are and start checking in with them regularly.

But before we explore your values, I'd like to introduce you to Natalie, Robert, and Mickey. Each had either outgrown values that once served them or were totally disregarding values that mattered most.

Misery Does Not Want Your Company

> *"Be grateful for all you receive, good and bad alike, for it may be*
> *a gift from the treasury of the Spirit that will bring the fulfillment*
> *of your most secret desire."*
>
> —Rumi's *Little Book of Life*

Natalie—Gutting It Out

Natalie sat across the table from me. It was a surprisingly comfortable late August day. Somehow, a breezy morning had slipped in between what had been a hot and muggy night and what would become a scorching afternoon.

"I've got to get out. I'm miserable. I dread going into work every day. I love my team, but I can't do this anymore. It's killing me," she fired off in rapid succession and the staccato pace continued. "Literally, I'm worried about my health. I'm taking meds for anxiety. I hate that. I come from a family where people die young."

Her eyes pleaded. The exhausted sighs punctuated her pain. The tears that she fought to control brought her more shame and embarrassment as they slipped down her cheeks. "I never cry. I can't believe I'm crying. I don't know what to do. It's seriously affecting my family. My partner is wonderful, so supportive, but I know the way everything is affecting me—it's not good. I don't know what to do."

I listened carefully to Natalie as she poured her suffering onto the outdoor patio table at the coffee shop where we had met. Her face creased with the stress of stuffing all that had been piled on her plate for too long.

Natalie spent her days in a high-stress leadership position where she raced hour after hour, jousting with problems, crises, staffing shortages, and an annual cycle of new bosses. At night she would lie awake wrestling with her decisions over this, remapping her conversations over that, and constantly second-guessing herself. She and her partner and their family of dogs lived in a lovely suburban community, but there was no time to enjoy it. For all that COVID-19 had brought in forced slowdowns, Natalie's life had returned to the pre-pandemic pace and the frantic unpredictability of a California wildfire, incinerating every fiber of her being and turning her soul to ashes.

Like many who find themselves in leadership roles, Natalie went into it thinking it was the appropriate next step and hoping everything would work out. But when she became a leader in her organization, she stopped leading herself. She gave over her power to a job—a career—that would greedily take it from her.

Ultimately, the giving and giving had left her dying inside. Although she had become a fragile and frustrated shell of her former strong, vibrant self, she was terrified to let go, set a new course, change her situation. For Natalie, the reasons to continue gutting it out were many and valid. "I make really good money." "I have a team of people that I need to take care of." "It's not fair to my partner." "I don't want 'them' to win." But something had to change.

Her values, she would discover, were shifting. Security, status, a sizeable income, and winning were still there, but they were far less important. New values—self-respect, calm, family—were emerging, and they were demanding to be honored.

Robert—Extreme Pressure

Robert was a big man from a small town. The former military brat and Army veteran had seen the world. But before the age of forty, he'd clocked three failed marriages, two heart attacks, and an extremely high-stress job that had taken its toll.

His face contorted with anger. His large, tattooed arms came to attention and his fists clenched with rage, as he described working for his former boss, a mean, hard, dirty, disrespectful, cruel man. Robert had seen and endured all of it. The years of working under extreme pressure in what felt like a constant state of fear and degradation had taken their toll.

His gigantic truck with the roaring engine screamed, "I take no shit from nobody!" Today, he wept as he told the story of missing his teenage son's high school graduation because the boss that he'd devoted years to insisted that he be at work. One of his most important values, family, had been the recurring casualty of his high-stress career.

Mickey—Slowly Disappearing

Mickey was a relatively new leader at thirty-five, when she described sitting in her therapist's office unable to breathe for having been seized by one of the frequent panic attacks that left her hyperventilating and visibly shaking as she tried to talk about her workplace situation. By the time she sought professional counseling, she had shrunk to eighty-eight pounds, couldn't sleep, and could barely eat. She was slowly disappearing.

The public sector organization where she had engaged in what was once meaningful and fulfilling work had become a haven for despair and a political hotbed of deception in which the newly elected and appointed officials arrived with their own agenda. It differed starkly from the organization's formerly altruistic mission. Quickly creating an environment of fear, the appointed leaders took to making false accusations against the senior staff, rank and file employees, and PhDs who had the audacity to push back and disagree with them. Politics may be a dirty, unethical game, but, for Mickey, it was as brutal as seeing baby seals being bludgeoned for sport.

Yet she hated the idea of "giving up." She had never been a quitter. She was driven, determined, tenacious, and was also on the verge of a breakdown. Grit was a value she held onto like a life raft, but it would drown her if she didn't loosen her grip.

Change Isn't What Happens. It Is What Is

While the toxic scenarios here may be hard to read and bitter to swallow, I'm sorry to say they are not uncommon. The 2023 Toxic Workplace Report revealed that, in a survey of two thousand employees across various industries, "a staggering 75 percent have experienced a toxic workplace culture."[33] As I noted in Chapter 5, toxic workplaces have enormous costs, billions of dollars in turnover, billions in lost productivity, tragic life-threatening errors, catastrophic safety violations, and decreased innovation, to name a few.

We can rightly lament the unfairness of it all. We can shake our collective heads and recall friends and family treated in horribly wrong and in unfair ways. We probably have our own painful memories of dreams lost and opportunities never realized. It's disheartening and it's wrong, I don't disagree. But that's not going to change the situation.

Even if the workplace isn't toxic, it's quite likely that there will come a time in which the job we loved, the career that was so fulfilling, the good organization where we had hoped to stay forever, the great team, or awesome boss no longer exists. Sometimes, it happens quickly. Other times, it's a gradual, almost invisible, erosion of what was. Yet we still cling tightly to the illusion that this shift, whatever it is, is just some temporary oversight,

---

[33] Oak Engage, Toxic Workplace Report 2023, https://www.oak.com/media/v1wp24tf/toxic-workplace-report-final-cleaned.pdf, p. 8

a blip in the matrix that is our well-planned professional life. Hoping and wishing and dreaming and praying, we tell ourselves that the situation will turn around. Weeks, months, even years may go by. But things are never going back to the way they once were.

Welcome to change. It is the nature of the world and the nature of work. Change isn't just what happens. It is what is. I'm not going to lie; Mother Nature's somewhat cruel joke is that while change truly is constant, we resist it at seemingly every turn. And when it arrives, usually at the most inopportune times, it feels like an unwelcome intruder banging on your front door. Do you invite them in, like Rumi's poem, *The Guest House*[34], and discover that perhaps they aren't intruders per se, but rather the fears and worries of the change that is and has been calling you? Perhaps behind those fears and worries there is opportunity, courage, adventure, and innovation. Or do you bolt the door tight and hope that these "intruders" and whatever message they are bringing just go away? It is up to you to decide how you are going to welcome change—or not. But it's always at your doorstep.

Your Values Are the Points on Your Compass

As *the* leader of Y-O-U, Inc., as well as *a* leader of your department, project, organization, requires you have a strong foundation of core values. In the often turbulent seas of challenge, change, and adversity, you must make thousands of decisions. Many are routine, a few are easy, others are difficult, and some have you searching your soul for direction. Clearly defined values are your guide. They are the points on your internal compass. Identifying them is part of taking responsibility for shaping your own identity and defining who you are.

You develop greater clarity around what you believe as a human and who you choose to be as a leader when you are anchored to your values in both

---

[34] Maryam Mafi and Azima Melita Kolin, *Rumi's Little Book of Life, The Garden of the Soul, the Heart, and the Spirit* (Charlottesville, VA: Hampton Roads Publishing Company, Inc., 2012) p. 16

challenging and calm times. They help nurture the culture you are creating on your team and in your organization. They shape your interactions with staff, clients, colleagues, family, and your community.

When it comes time to explore new opportunities, to walk away from destructive work situations, to choose to set out on our own, to pursue dreams, our values light the way. Yet, few new leaders give attention to their core values until they find themselves looking out from the cage they built for themselves and are unhappy with the job, career, relationship, circumstance, or important decision and wondering how they got there. Get to know your values. They are your guide, your sherpa, your advisor, especially when the winds of change start kicking up.

The exercises that follow are designed to help you get clarity on what's truly important to you as a person, a professional, and a leader.

What You Don't Tell Yourself Is as Important as What You Do

When I work with clients, I begin with a series of questions. These help me better understand what the client really values beyond the buzzwords and beneath the things that they think they "should" say they value.

I've included a version of the questions here in the 10-Question Self-Portrait. Set some time aside to reflect on and answer the questions. Keep it real. Your answers should be honest and free of judgment.

Once you've answered the questions, go back and review your responses. Read between the lines of what you've written. Notice what you tell yourself and what you're choosing to ignore or step over in your answers. Those thoughts that emerge that you're hesitant to write down are the loudspeaker blasting what's really important to you. Pay attention. There are no right or wrong values. What's happening at any given personal and professional stage can have a significant influence on what we value during the different seasons of our lives and careers.

Your answers help you to paint a picture of your values at this time. You may find that the snapshot you reveal to yourself is one that those around you would benefit from seeing as well.

Your 10-Question Self-Portrait

The following questions are intended to be reflective. Take your time with them and write down your answers.

1. What five things do you wish people knew about you?

2. What in life is most important to you?

3. What things give you enjoyment?

4. What is it about those things that give you joy?

5. What are your biggest achievements so far?

6. What are the beliefs, strengths, and patterns of behavior that enabled those achievements?

7. What are your dreams/goals/aspirations—professionally and personally?

8. What are the biggest challenges you face in reaching and/or moving toward your dreams/goals/aspirations?

9. What are you avoiding as a leader right now and why?

10. What is your greatest fear and how do you deal with it?

For new or newer leaders in particular, the question "What is your greatest fear?" will often be answered with the word "failure." This is an opportunity to look at what is truly frightening about failure.

How do you define failure? Is it missing an Oxford comma in a routine document or making a life and death decision? A fear of failure may be an indication that you value high standards and strong attention to detail. Or you may work for an exacting perfectionist who's sucking the joy from Y-O-U, Inc.

There could be any number of other reasons that surround a fear of failure. Getting clear on the motivation beneath the answers to this and the other questions helps you better understand if your responses truly represent values that you hold, or if your answers might be reflecting expectations that have been thrust upon you. Your values must be yours, what's important to you fundamentally, not rooted in what you think others think they should be.

Another area that can be very revealing is the question about what leaders wish people knew about them. New leaders may report that they wish others knew they care deeply about an important issue, their team, or that they'd experienced a significant loss that sometimes makes it difficult for them to connect with their teammates. These answers, like others, often reveal the veins of important underlying values.

What do your responses tell you about what you value at this time?

Values Clarity in Seven Steps

Another tool you can use to begin to explore your values is the Values Inventory. Full disclosure, I'm not a huge fan of just picking values from a list for two reasons. One, no matter how "good" the list is, it will not be totally comprehensive, and two, plucking a few values off a list and claiming them as yours doesn't allow for much self-reflection. So, to make the Values Inventory selection process more real and meaningful, it's important to spend time on the steps listed below.

1. Review the list of values that follows. Use it as inspiration, not limitation. You're not restricted to just these seventy words. Feel free to add to the list, combine words, make up your own. Highlight or underline those words that resonate with you.

2. Next, from the inspiration words you've highlighted and your answers to the 10-Question Self-Portrait, make a list of your top ten values.

3. Beside each value, write down why it is important to you.

4. Next, write a sentence that describes how you demonstrate each value you've selected in action.

5. Narrow the list to your top seven, better yet, your top five, if possible.

6. During each day next week, choose a different value from your list and pay attention to how you demonstrate this value in your actions, interactions, decisions, choices, thoughts, and behaviors.

7. Consider if different values are emerging that perhaps you didn't recognize or expect when you crafted your original list, or are you finding that some values in your top five list are continually getting pushed to the side in favor of others? How might you bring more balance to honoring these other important values?

1. Accountable
2. Adaptable
3. Ambitious
4. Assertive
5. Authentic
6. Balance
7. Caring
8. Collaboration
9. Commitment
10. Compassion
11. Continuous Learning
12. Courage
13. Critical Thinking
14. Curiosity
15. Customer Focus
16. Detail-oriented
17. Disciplined
18. Efficiency
19. Empathy
20. Empowerment
21. Enthusiasm
22. Excellence
23. Fairness
24. Freedom
25. Generosity
26. Gratitude
27. Growth
28. Honest
29. Humble
30. Inclusive
31. Independent

32. Innovative
33. Inspiring
34. Integrity
35. Intuitive
36. Joy
37. Justice
38. Kind
39. Leader
40. Loving
41. Loyal
42. Open
43. Optimistic
44. Patient
45. Passionate
46. Perseverance
47. Professional
48. Profitable
49. Quality
50. Reliable
51. Resourceful
52. Resilient
53. Respectful
54. Responsible
55. Risk Avoider
56. Risk Taker
57. Safety
58. Service
59. Security
60. Strategic
61. Sustainability
62. Teamwork
63. Transparent
64. Trustworthy
65. Unity
66. Unflinching
67. Unique
68. Willful
69. Wise
70. Wonder

Where Your Attention Goes, Energy Flows

Put your list of top five values somewhere that you can see them daily and easily—on a whiteboard, Post-it Note on your computer, screen saver on your phone, etc. As challenges, changes, and decisions confront you, consider how you might respond through the lens of each core value.

When you sense that it's time to explore a new opportunity, leave your current job, change careers, start your own business, make a difficult decision, or whatever seemingly scary move is tugging at you, spend time with your top five list. Perhaps your value of "loyal" has served you well in your role, but another value, "innovative," is calling you to make a change. Your values are the quiet whisper that keeps nudging you forward. Hear them out.

Natalie, Robert, Mickey

Natalie agonized over her decision to leave the organization where she'd spent much of her career. During a leave of absence, it became abundantly clear that she needed to make a shift. The move was frightening and far from perfect. The first job she took was not fulfilling and felt like a step backward. After just eight months, she took a much more rewarding position that has allowed her to use her many leadership strengths and grow professionally in an ancillary field. Today, she is thriving and loves her new career. She honors her values of connection, self-care, continuous learning, and family.

Robert continues to work in an extremely high-stress industry. He does not believe that he can find a job that does not require him to work sixty-hour weeks. He has little time or energy for his family and remains very unhappy.

Mickey went into business for herself and is flourishing. The lessons that she learned working in a highly toxic organization were some of the most valuable of her career. Today, she checks in with her values regularly. She has significant clarity around the types of clients she will accept in her business and those she will not.

Let Go and Leave on Good Terms

> *"The most difficult thing is the decision to act,*
> *the rest is merely tenacity."*
>
> —Amelia Earhart

The time has come. Things have changed. You're ready for new challenges. You have bigger dreams and goals that you're ready to pursue.

Your values are calling you in a different direction. You want more time with your family or to travel or go back to school, or perhaps you find yourself dreading going to work. You're in a constant state of high stress. Your self-confidence has bottomed out. You've made a genuine effort to make this job work, it isn't. Whatever the reason, you've accepted that you and this organization are no longer a good fit for each other.

It's time to make your exit. Do so with grace and respect. Do NOT burn bridges. Here are a few practical points to keep in mind as you close this door and open the next.

1. Give a *minimum* of two weeks' notice in writing. Be respectful and try to be appreciative. This is not the time to air your grievances or point fingers. Even if you didn't love the job or if things soured along the way, you grew, you learned, and you earned a paycheck.

You can also use your resignation letter to point out a few of the accomplishments that you're most proud of as a new leader.

For example:

> *Dear Boss, Thank you for the opportunity to be part of the Widget team for the past three years. I have accepted a new position and my last day with Widget will be March 31. During my remaining time here, I will do everything I can to ensure a smooth transition.*
>
> *I have learned a great deal and sincerely appreciated the opportunity to be part of the Widget organization. I'm honored to have played a role in some exciting initiatives during my time here, including: a. b. c.*
>
> *I wish you and the Widget team the very best.*

In addition to leaving on good terms and extending appreciation, including a few highlights of your accomplishments makes it easy for your former boss to cite some of your contributions should you use them as a reference in the future.

2. Tell your boss that you're leaving before you tell anyone else inside or outside the company—except maybe your spouse. Your boss may want to make the announcement or, at a minimum, inform their leader.

3. Set up your team for success. Provide details on projects, share all relevant files and information pertaining to projects you've been leading or working on.

4. Set up your replacement for success. List your responsibilities, contacts, projects, etc.

5. Don't check out before you walk out. Make it clear what you will wrap up before your last day. Continue to show up with energy and commitment to the work and the organization. Complete the projects and assignments that you've committed to finishing.

6. Keep the exit interview professional, candid, and express gratitude for the experience. Communicate the facts of your experience neutrally and constructively.

7. Pay attention to the details of your departure, namely how much the company owes you in salary, vacation, unused sick time, retirement, etc.

Run Toward, Not Away

The decision to leave a job or change careers is seldom, if ever, easy. But what is easy is to become consumed by the negativity and focus squarely on what you're running from—the bad boss, the unethical culture, the difficult team, the unfair decisions, etc. The "I just want to get out of here" mindset may give you temporary relief, but it probably won't get you to where you want or need to be. Most likely, it will have you jumping from the proverbial frying pan into the fire.

Check in with your values. Make a list of your non-negotiables. Get clear on what you really want 6, 12, 24 months from now. Visualize what you are running toward. What do you want to create? What does your next job, opportunity, position look like, feel like, sound like? Focus not on what you don't want, but rather on what you do want in the next phase of your life's journey. Then start crafting your strategy. Update your resume, create your plan and map your next steps. Remember you are the leader and CEO of Y-O-U, Inc.

And Finally

As challenges and changes ebb and flow, keep this in mind: The trees do not stomp their roots in protest as the sweeping winds brazenly strip bare their branches. The moon doesn't curse the sun as it rises to take its place each morning. The caterpillar doesn't protest the butterfly any more than the seed laments the fruit. Change is what is. Welcome it, for this seemingly dreaded and difficult experience may just "bring the fulfillment of your secret desire."

ABOUT THE AUTHOR

Tess Fyalka, PCC, CPCC, ACTC, is a leadership development coach, team coach, corporate trainer, speaker, and author. She brings more than twenty-five years' experience in leadership, management, corporate training, and organizational development. Tess has worked with leaders in multiple industries. And her passion is helping leaders at all levels develop the essential core competencies to lead successfully and equipping organizational teams with the tools they need to cut through challenging team dynamics and achieve their full potential. She is the owner of Angle Coaching & Communication, LLC (www.anglecoaching.com), a private coaching and consulting practice specializing in leadership development and team effectiveness.